W9-BBA-161

What Happened at Rome?

Gary MacEoin

What
Happened
at Rome?

*The Council
and its
Implications
for the
Modern
World*

Introduction by John Cogley

Holt, Rinehart and Winston
New York   Chicago   San Francisco

Designer: Ernst Reichl
85418–0216
Printed in the United States of America

Acknowledgments

Hundreds of people in fifty different countries, many of them without knowing it, helped me to write this book. They include Archbishop Finbar Ryan, Port-of-Spain, Trinidad; Edward Kirchner, Stamford, Connecticut; Metropolitan Chrysostomos of Myra, Istanbul; Father Xavier Eid, Cairo; Gus Madden, Rome; Father Thomas Hopkins, St. Chad's Anglican Mission, South Africa; Patricia and John Boyne, Dublin; Jean-Pierre Dubois-Dumée, Paris; Father Johannes Düsing, Jerusalem; Malek Al-Samarrie, Baghdad; Father Luis López, Aizu Wakamatsu, Japan; Dom Helder Camara, Brazil; Bernard Daly, Ottawa, Canada; Antonio Paternó di Sessa, Milan; Father Ciaran Tormey, Rome; Nan and Sigmund Eisner, San Francisco; Martha Mistretta, Nutley, New Jersey; Father François Houtart, Belgium; Herbert Auhofer, Germany; Richard Senier, Boston; Joseph Cunneen, New York; Father Daniel O'Hanlon, California; Madge and Phil Bagnall, Dublin; Bishop Sergio Méndez Arceo, Cuernavaca, Mexico; Eleanor Shank, Hong Kong; Father Pierre Duprey, Rome; Mary Daly, Fribourg, Switzerland; Father Martin MacManus, Abakaliki, Nigeria; Father Francis Xavier Murphy, Rome; Jerzy Turowicz, Poland; Father Emile Gabel, Paris; Pat Keegan, London; Robert Kaiser, Los Angeles; Father Ambrose McNicholl, Rome; Bishop Joseph Blomjous, Mwanza, Tanzania. An even greater debt than to these and to the many others whose names go unrecorded I owe to Angelo Roncalli, Pope John XXIII.

To my wife

with love, affection, and thanks

Contents

Introduction

In some Catholic circles one is supposed to say that nothing fundamental was changed by the Second Vatican Council. The dutiful Catholic journalist or pulpit apologist is expected to insist that the Church that went into council in October, 1962, and the one that came out in December, 1965, were essentially the same.

The trick word here of course is "essentially." If it is used in a certain way and given a certain philosophical emphasis, the statement is unexceptionable. For Vatican II did not break the Catholic continuity between the Church of Jerusalem at the time of the Lord's ascension and the Church whose bishops assembled in Rome in the early 1960's. Still, the differences between the Church of Peter I and that of Paul VI are obvious. History and the passage of time have wrought changes in the Catholic Church that would have been unimaginable to the immediate followers of St. Peter, however much its Catholic "essence" has gone untouched.

It is with such changes as this that Mr. MacEoin deals in *What Happened at Rome?* His is the approach of the journalist and, at his best, sometimes that of the historian. A good journalist puts almost scandalous stress on the existential, the visible, the phenomenological; he is perhaps less interested in such final categories as essence and substance than in the texture of life and its everyday meaning. Mr. MacEoin, let it be said, is a superb journalist.

During the Vatican Council Rome was full of distinguished journalists from both the religious and the secular press. A number, I have no doubt, were just as skilled as Gary MacEoin in collecting facts and setting them forth with coherence and insight. Some perhaps write prose as graceful.

Still, I doubt that any of the rest of us who showed up at the press conferences day after day could have written *What Happened at Rome?* The reason it needed Mr. MacEoin, I believe, is because he has been preparing to write this book all his life.

I do not mean that the preparation was conscious—he could hardly have readied himself to report on an ecumenical council that no one anticipated—but it well may have been providential. The special background and experience Mr. MacEoin brought with him to Rome were almost ideal endowments for anyone trying to make sense out of the incoherencies, accomplishments, setbacks, struggles, and final conclusions of the Second Vatican Council.

To understand what happened in Rome, one had to be familiar not only with the doctrinal teachings of the Catholic Church but with the theological and philosophical mode in which these teachings have been traditionally and authoritatively put forth. This was the stumbling block for many journalists.

Moreover, one had to be familiar not only with universal Catholicity but with the manifold expressions of the same basic religious beliefs in a dozen different Catholicisms. Most of us were limited here. We knew the Catholicism of our own land, with its particularities; but we were generally untutored in the differences between, say, the Church in Pittsburgh and the Church in Bogota.

Mr. MacEoin, an inveterate traveler, familiar with the Church on several continents, had the edge. Long before the Vatican Council began, he had acquired a background by interviewing leading prelates the world over. He had a detailed knowledge of specific problems facing the Church in different lands, as well as a sensitive feeling for the variations that distinguish Catholicism from place to place.

Others of us knew, for example, that Catholicism in the Middle West of the United States and the Catholicism found on the eastern seaboard were distinct entities; we could also see that American Catholicism and what was before our eyes in Italy were different. But few if any had the variety of Gary MacEoin's immediate experiences with the Church at the earth's four corners.

When he watched the bishops of various nations and races walking into St. Peter's, he had a livelier sense than most of us of the social and even theological value-systems, the predilections and prejudices they were bringing with them. He could see the schema on religious liberty, to take one instance, through the eyes not only of a New York prelate brought up on the tolerant streets of Manhattan but of an aristocratic but benighted Latin American prelate who may never have met a live Protestant in his whole life, or a long-unchallenged Irish bishop who held fast to the textbook certitudes in a changing world.

If the term "Catholic journalist" has any meaning other than to designate one who writes continually for the church press or to single out one who is publicly known as a member of the Catholic Church, then Gary MacEoin is the Catholic journalist par excellence.

His interest in Catholic affairs has not lagged through years of travel and ever-broadening knowledge of the world. Years ago in an Irish classroom he might have been taught to see the Church as an almost Platonic ideal, an abstract theological conception. But a journalistic sense developed over the years soon accustomed him to view it as a living reality, moving and breathing and having its being in the incarnational mode, in a dozen different ways around the globe.

Mr. MacEoin, always a mild-mannered man, with no known tendency to raise his voice, is stupendously sophisticated about Catholicism. Nothing in the Church surprises him, it would seem: While he holds out for the highest standards from the Church and her people, his expectations in the concrete order might seem to some to be minimal. Perhaps that is why for years he has been saying things in the Catholic press that, when they were said by others, brought on violent reactions. He has mysteriously avoided being known as an Angry Layman. Yet a reading of this book on the Council will show that he pulls no punches and does not hesitate to point a finger of blame or of scorn when he feels it is necessary.

I expected something milder when I was first asked to read the manuscript for *What Happened at Rome?* I must confess, too, that I was not particularly anxious to get at it. I had, it seemed, read dozens of books about the Council, though actually I suppose the number was more like six or seven. I had been reporting on it three years straight for months at a time. It was the standard topic of social conversation in conciliar Rome. The idea of reading one more book about it had no appeal whatsoever.

However, after I got into Mr. MacEoin's work, my enthusiasm for it grew. I liked what I found. I liked the generally low-key journalistic approach to a subject frequently handled with apostolic passion or reformer's zeal. I also liked the wealth of background the author brought to his task, ranging from sociological information through theological and philosophical briefings to effortless historical references.

I would not say that Mr. MacEoin has written the best book about Vatican II. In my view a number of the books already published were excellent. Xavier Rynne's informative volumes were a major contribution, despite the extreme partisanship that sometimes marred them. Michael Novak's brilliant *The Open Church* transcended its immediate aim—to report on the second session—and turned out to be a major statement of a contemporary Catholic outlook. Robert Blair Kaiser's *Time*-ly account of the first session was journalism of a high order. Gary MacEoin's book takes its place with volumes like these. It is not for me to assign any order of priority of excellence to them.

What Mr. MacEoin has written, however, is the book that I wish I had written. The reason I say that, I suppose, is purely professional. If one gives one's life to journalism—"mere journalism" as it is frequently called in the Academy—simple unadorned communication becomes a highly valued goal. When it is necessary to move above the sheer level of fact and communicate the meaning and significance of great spiritual movements and historic forces, then the journalistic task becomes more difficult. The arts required for it are of a subtle nature.

Anyone reporting on the Vatican Council had the latter task. A mere recital of what was said and by whom, when, and where could communicate little of the Council's genuine significance. Religious reporting, as I believe many learned during the four autumns the Council was in session, requires certain gifts and understandings that are not readily available in every city room.

Mr. MacEoin in his own quiet way has such gifts in abundance. Accepting the entire four sessions of Vatican II as his assignment, he undertakes to communicate not merely what happened in Rome but the meaning of what happened for the world-wide Church. I believe he succeeds.

To understand what happened requires a minute knowledge of the pre-Johannine Church as well as a share in the vision of the bishops and theologians who hoped that the Council Pope John called would be the source of true Catholic reformation and renewal. Again, life prepared Mr. MacEoin for his assignment.

I suppose every journalist who covered Vatican II was tempted at some time to write a book. Most, I feel sure, must have been approached by one publisher or another. I was both tempted and approached. For reasons that seemed right to me, however, I resisted, not without regret, mingled with the relief that I would not be trying to say what had already been said so well.

Now I am glad I said no. For Gary MacEoin has written the book I wish I could have written. If I did have a manuscript ready for the printer, it would have been discouraging to know that what I had done had already been done much better.

JOHN COGLEY

New York
March 1966

What Happened at Rome?

Chapter 1

The
Council Begins

St. Peter's Square, Rome, was the scene of a unique pageant on December 8, 1965. It marked the closing of the Second Vatican Council, the 21st general council of the Catholic Church in the 19 centuries of its existence.

The spectacle was witnessed by 20,000 pilgrims and sightseers in the piazza and several thousand privileged guests who jammed windows, balconies, galleries, and roof gardens. Television carried it around the world into millions of living rooms. Some who watched were edified by the manifestation of living faith, the proclamation of rededication to service of God and of mankind. Others were fascinated by the pageantry. Many asked themselves what it all meant.

Nearly seven years earlier, Pope John made an offhand announcement that he was thinking of summoning an ecumenical council. "An ecumenical council, what's that?" Such was the usual reaction to the news, even among Catholics. Indifference increased over the following years as a dozen committees in Rome sifted in elaborate secrecy tens of thousands of suggestions from all over the world. It was obviously going to be a very churchy affair conducted within the rigid framework of Roman discretion.

The Council met on October 11, 1962. A Central Committee of 102 cardinals and bishops had waded through 140 docu-

3

ments drafted by 10 commissions and the Secretariat for Christian Unity and had picked 70 for discussion. The documents ranged over every likely and unlikely subject from revelation through ecclesiastical benefices to spiritualism and reincarnation. How could the Fathers deal with such an agenda? Predictions were confidently made that it would be a rubber-stamp Council.

Then things began to happen. The first order of business was to elect the members of the all-important working committees. Cardinal Liénart of France challenged the official lists of candidates. Cardinal Frings of Germany backed him. There was scattered applause. The Fathers looked at one another. The applause spread. It was agreed by acclamation to adjourn for informal discussions leading to more representative lists.

"Bishops in revolt" screamed the forgivably inaccurate headlines. The world was shocked, then elated. Everyone wanted more information. The Council had ceased to be an internal Catholic affair. Protestants began to ask how it was likely to modify and hopefully improve their relations with their Catholic neighbors. What would the new emphases, the new issues, be?

The session continued until December 8 without providing clear answers. Not a single document was given final approval. Indeed, only one received a friendly reception, a project of reform of the liturgy, or official prayer, of the Church. It sought to restore the emphasis of the early Church on Christ as the center of worship, upgraded the sense of community, stressed the importance of active participation of the faithful, and made this easier by substituting the local language for Latin.

The other 69 projects were rejected outright or sent back for rewriting and consolidation. But the session was not wasted. The mind of the Council was firmly established, for example, in the debate on revelation. By a vote of 1,368 to 822, the Fathers rejected a document drafted in polemical terms to insist against the Protestants that Scripture and Tradition constituted two distinct sources of revelation. Pope John showed his approval by short-circuiting procedural rules and ordering a total rewriting.

In addition, the bishops got to know one another. Names from distant places grew familiar and important: Blomjous of Tanganyika, Helder Camara of Brazil, Nagae of Japan, Maximos IV Saïgh of Antioch, D'Souza of India, Zoa of Equatorial Africa. It became increasingly apparent that the progressive leaders (as the press was starting to call them)—Belgium's Suenens, Germany's Frings, Holland's Alfrink, and Austria's König—had a world-wide following.

The Council faced a new crisis when Pope John died on June 3, 1963. Would his successor continue with the project, and would he allow equal freedom of debate and decision? Cardinal Montini was known to have been favored by John to succeed him, and Montini's election was considered a good omen. He quickly answered the first question by fixing September 29 to begin a new session. The answer to the other question emerged gradually. Paul would intervene more than John and would sometimes irritate by his manner of intervention. But in the main, he would give the bishops their head.

The nine-week second session brought the first concrete results. Two documents were finally approved, one on liturgical reform, the other on communications media. The rest of the encyclopedic program was streamlined and centered around two great themes—a study of the Church's nature and a study of its relations with the contemporary world. It had become clear that very many Fathers favored change. This did not necessarily make them liberals in any sense of the word. Some were motivated largely by irritation at the overcentralization of authority in Rome. But at least they were willing to back a program for more internal freedom and a greater participation of the laity in the Church's life. They also agreed on a new attitude of friendship toward other Christians and a desire for ultimate reunion, as well as an affirmation of the positive content of Judaism, Islam, Hinduism, and the other great religions of the world. This program, identified as "progressive," would consistently win the support of more than 90 per cent of the Fathers, many of whom would in other respects change few of their conservative ways. It would also be fought at all points and by every available means by the small minority strongly entrenched in the Church's central government in Rome.

A third session, from September 14 to November 21, 1964, brought the decisive victory of the progressives with the passage of the statements on the nature of the Church and on ecumenism. But the opposition did not surrender. Only one further document was voted on at this session. Backstage maneuvers prevented decisive action on two key texts, one presenting the Church's position on religious freedom, the other on its attitude toward the Jews. The session closed in a pall of gloom when Pope Paul sided with the conservative minority on several important issues.

The fourth session convened on September 14, 1965. Everyone was happy that it would be the last. Episcopal fatigue had set in. The progressives recognized that they had advanced just about as far as was prudent for the time being, that a period of consolidation and assimilation was indicated. The conservatives likewise realized that they lacked the strength for a major counteroffensive, that they could hope at most to occupy some minor salients. Both groups had sufficient respect and love for the Church to shy away from a showdown that might end the Council in a debacle.

The final session, accordingly, moved along at a business-like pace. Eleven documents were approved, completing the agenda. They included a 30,000-word review of the place and function of the Church in the world, a first attempt at dialogue with contemporary man. They also included statements on the Jews and on religious freedom, both scarred by their passage through the debating chamber, yet generally regarded as not substantially eviscerated. Various committees were set up to carry out decisions made by the Council. Responding to a request of the Fathers, the pope created a new body that would meet periodically to review Church policy. Most of its members would be elected by the bishops all over the world.

The Council was over, but after years of soul-searching by the 2,500 top leaders of the largest Christian denomination, after more than 300 hours of speeches, several tons of written suggestions, some 500 votes, and 16 promulgated documents, was the Catholic Church still in the Middle Ages? Was the spectacle of the closing ceremony what the Church understood by the *aggiornamento*, the updating, for which Pope John had called? Did it see no incongruity in presenting the pope, borne like a medieval monarch on the shoulders of his vassals and flanked by his helmeted troops? Did it think that substituting a gold-plated ring for a jeweled one eliminated the sole obstacle to dialogue between a Catholic bishop and a man of the twentieth century?

Such questions were not easy to answer. The press had given sympathetic and substantial coverage to the Council from the beginning. It had stressed the Council's desire to avoid repeating condemnations, its support for the principle of religious freedom, its rejection of anti-Semitism, its efforts to work more closely with Protestants and other Christians, its concern for the underdeveloped world, its re-evaluation of the Church's attitudes on family limitation.

The Council had indeed attempted all these things. But on almost every issue it had seemed to fall just short of its objective. It was obvious that most Catholics desired significant change, that most of the bishops at the Council similarly wanted it. But behind-the-scenes forces of opposition never gave up the struggle. They had suffered major setbacks in the early stages, had survived, rallied, and staged a remarkable comeback. Were they still in control? And when the bishops had scattered to the four corners of the globe, would the same forces draw a velvet curtain over the brief unhappy episode and restore the image and the reality of the monolithic centralized control that had characterized the Catholic Church for centuries?

That all these questions could be asked was itself a significant measure of the progress achieved by the Council. Before Pope John, they were unthinkable. And even when he first talked about a council, few suspected that it would open up the extraordinary range of self-examination that it did, still less that it would reveal the depth of the latent desire for change.

To say this does not mean that before Pope John there was no internal concern about the condition and position of the Catholic Church. At least some were aware that Catholics were a small and dwindling minority in the world, persecuted in Communist states, facing restrictions in the new states of the postcolonial regions, unable to meet the material and spiritual needs of nominally Catholic Latin America. They knew that the Church's teachings were regarded as irrelevant by many for whom science offered the explanation and justification of existence, that growing numbers of men preferred the Communist to the Christian explanation of struggle and suffering.

But before John, even those Catholics who were aware of Catholicism's defensive posture saw no alternative to the official policy that had been in effect for four centuries since the Protestant Reformation. They agreed, at least in public, that the Church was a militant group mobilized on a war basis to fight the battles of the Lord, regardless of odds or results. Setbacks, such as those occurring and anticipated, called for a progressively tighter administrative centralization. To challenge official policy was to give aid and comfort to the enemy, an act of treason in time of war.

Then, at the least-expected moment, the view changed sharply. In 1958, Pius XII died, full of years and honor. His reign and that of his predecessor, Pius XI, had spanned 36 years. It had been a period of strict adherence to an undeviating line of policy, so obviously right as to call for its indefinite continuance. But when the cardinals assembled to elect a new pope, no candidate appeared ideally suited to follow in the footsteps of the two Piuses. Lacking a clear-cut choice, the cardinals did what papal electors had often done in the past. They opted for an interim pope, one whose years and qualities guaranteed a brief and untroubled breathing spell. And precisely such a one was at hand. Angelo Giuseppe Roncalli was 77 years old, genial, and corpulent. His long years of faithfully inconspicuous service in the Vatican's diplomatic corps had been duly rewarded six years earlier with a red hat and the diocese of Venice.

Roncalli raised some eyebrows right away. He picked a name which had been avoided for hundreds of years because it had been borne by one pope of suspect theological views and another whose claim to the papacy was doubtful. Suspicions that John XXIII was not following the script were quickly confirmed. On January 25, 1959, he casually informed a group of 18 or 19 cardinals that he was going to call a general council.

The last thing the Curia, the Church's central administrative body, wanted was to have several thousand bishops tell it what was good for the Church. Particularly after the definition of papal infallibility at the Vatican Council in 1870, it had become a well-established practice for the Curia, in the name and with the authority of the supreme pontiff, to tell the bishops what was good for the Church. The 1917 Code of Canon Law reflected this view in its ranking of the Church hierarchy as pope, ecumenical synod, cardinals, Roman Curia, legates of the pope, patriarchs, archbishops and metropolitans, bishops . . .

Then began what was literally a race against death, even if at the time the protagonists were not aware of just how numbered John's days were. Could the preparations be made so elaborate as to postpone the Council opening until nature took its course with the unexpectedly troublesome old pope? Failing that, could the bishops be maneuvered into rubber-stamping decisions made in advance by the Curia? The alternative possibility was demonstrated when the local synod of Rome met in January 1960. Summoned by John to give a new look to his own diocese, and hailed by the Curia-controlled *Osservatore Romano* as a preview of the Council, it tamely accepted a rehash of the long-sanctioned articles of war.

As yet, little evidence had come to light of any significant desire within the Church for a serious change of tactics and policies. John had been far from specific about his intentions, but they are well summarized in a phrase frequently attributed to him. He said he wanted "to open a window and let in a little fresh air." His first public expression of his idea for the Council was not much more precise. The purpose of the Council, he told a group of cardinals in January 1959, would be "to proclaim the truth, bring Christians closer to the faith, and contribute at the same time to peace and prosperity on earth." The words might have been used by any pope; somehow, when John used them, they had new overtones.

John was well aware that a deep ferment of discontent and dissatisfaction was at work within the Church. He was determined to bring it to the surface and utilize it as a leaven of renewal. One of his first steps in preparing the Council was to invite views from all sides. Soon, thousands of proposals and suggestions came flooding in on Rome, not the anonymous outpourings of cranks but the formulated requests of cardinals, bishops, and theologians. If there was yet no clear focus, the range of criticisms revealed the existence of frustrations that hitherto none had dared whisper.

Curial control of expression of opinion kept most of this criticism from public knowledge during the period of preparation. But as soon as the first session of the Council began in

October 1962, the facts had to be faced. The critical confrontation occurred at the very first work meeting on October 13, 1962. Cardinal Liénart of France and Cardinal Frings of Germany successfully challenged the pre-selection of the members of 10 committees that would have a decisive voice in the proceedings. The Curia tried hard to hide from the outside world both the existence of a conflict and the nature of the issues. But a point of no return had been reached. The pattern of the Council had been set, a contest between two intrinsically irreconcilable points of view. Techniques of secrecy could not conceal a fact of such dimensions. Its dynamic implications were soon a matter of universal knowledge.

At the United Nations, or in almost any contemporary national assembly, the issue would be resolved by a majority vote. The conventions of an ecumenical council are more complicated. The Fathers strive for what is called moral unanimity. They avoid a showdown until it is clear that an overwhelming majority has agreed on the issue. The concept is a subtle one, capable of significant political manipulation, and while it has obvious advantages, it encourages a solving of differences by way of compromise, a process in which the original principles can become so watered down or distorted as to become scarcely recognizable. If the primary purpose is to keep all the members of the assembly happy, it becomes easy to forget that the underlying purpose of the assembly is to advance the common good.

The important part played by these attitudes in the decisions of Vatican II is well illustrated by the history of the proposal to formulate the attitude of Catholics toward Jews. A theologically minor issue, at least as compared with the Council's effort to define the nature of the Church or the meaning of divine revelation, it nevertheless showed how complicated is the process of change in a body so old and so widely distributed geographically as the Catholic Church.

It all began quietly enough. Pope John had suggested that one of the main tasks of the Council would be to prepare the way for Christians to unite. To further the project, he established, in 1960, an organization called the Secretariat for Promoting Christian Unity and named a German Jesuit, Cardinal Bea, as its head. Bea was the ideal choice for the job. An outstanding Scripture scholar admired by progressives yet respected by conservatives, he combined a diplomatic manner with untiring drive. Still more, he understood what John wanted, and he loved him for wanting it.

The immediate reaction to the creation of the secretariat to promote better relations with other Christians was so favorable that John decided he should also do something about Catholic attitudes toward non-Christians. The logical place to start was with the Jews. Their religion was closer to Christianity than any other. In addition, the bitter persecutions they had known in the twentieth century demonstrated the need for better understanding on the part of the Christian world.

In 1961, accordingly, John asked Bea to prepare a statement for study by the upcoming Council on Catholic attitudes toward the Jews. The Cardinal was very happy to co-operate. The experience of his homeland had taught him that prejudice against the Jews was widespread among Catholics, and that it had played a significant part in the Nazi-led persecutions of the Jews. As a Scripture scholar, he knew how one-sided interpretations of the scriptural accounts of the Crucifixion had helped to feed anti-Semitism.

The statement that reached the Council in November 1963 reflected this concrete understanding of anti-Semitism. It demolished the claim that the Jews as a people were deicides or had been cursed by Christ. By a skillful use of scriptural texts, it made it clear that a limited group of Jews, not representative of popular feeling, had brought about Christ's death. These leaders had taken the precaution not to move on the day of the festival, because they feared that the assembled people would rise to defend Christ. Nor was there unanimity even among the leaders. Joseph of Arimathea, for example, had not been a party to the plans of his colleagues. Ignorance, moreover, had reduced the culpability even of those who had conspired to have Jesus killed. He himself said so with His dying breath, and both Peter and Paul repeated Christ's statement in their preaching. In addition, the first Christians were almost all Jews, and Paul had declared most explicitly that God had not rejected His chosen people and that the whole of Israel would finally find salvation. "A partial blindness only has befallen Israel," Paul wrote to the Romans, "until the full number of the Gentiles should enter, and thus all Israel should be saved" (11:25).

This rectification and re-evaluation of history offered a vision worthy of the generous mind of Pope John. Christianity emerged less as a rejection than as a refinement of Judaism. Christians were reminded that the Jews were the recipients and remain the guardians of God's first revelation to mankind. For that very reason, their religion is in a category quite different from all other non-Christian religions.

The storms of protest raised by the distribution of the Bea draft demonstrated the depth of the prejudice it was designed to counter. Privately printed pamphlets circulated among the Fathers repeated the traditional charges and argued that it was not only a Catholic's right but his duty to be anti-Jewish. The pseudonymous Bernardus in one such pamphlet ("The Jews and the Council") surveyed a long list of papal documents to establish that the papacy had already ruled decisively on the issue. For some the pamphlet had an effect opposite to that intended by its compilers, demonstrating as it did that the Church had ample reason to make amends. Yet it carried weight with those who held that any position established by the clear practice of Rome over a long period of time was irreversible. It was a point that would arise many times during the Council (on birth control, for example), and it would always arouse the most impassioned reactions.

Much stress has been laid on external political pressures designed to kill the statement on the Jews. They were highlighted in the Council debates. Cardinal Tappouni, Syrian Patriarch of Antioch, Cardinal Maximos IV Saïgh, Greek-Melchite Patriarch of Antioch, and others from Arab countries warned that Christians living in Moslem lands would suffer because the statement would be interpreted politically as favoring the State of Israel. Their opposition, they insisted, was not inspired by anti-Semitism. On the contrary, as some pointed out, they were themselves Semites. But, they said, a sentence would suffice to repudiate anti-Semitism. It did not need the prominence that Cardinal Bea proposed.

One does not have to question the good faith of these spokesmen of the Christians of the Near East. No matter how much the Council might emphasize that its intention was nonpolitical, the distinction has little meaning for the Islamic countries in which the civil and the religious are inextricably mixed. In addition, there is in all the Near East a strong tradition of anti-Jewish feeling among Christians, both Orthodox and Catholic. It exists not only at the popular level but also among theologians, who bolster it by arguments based on scriptural passages and on "tradition." So intense is the feeling that it has been exploited in Syria, for example, to persuade Eastern-rite Catholics to go over to the Orthodox, on the grounds that the Council was abandoning Catholic teaching by "rehabilitating" the Jews.

Other attempts to scuttle the statement were less understandable. Pamphlets distributed to the Council Fathers included one entitled "The Jewish-Masonic Action in the Council." It charged Cardinal Bea with taking orders from B'nai B'rith, and insinuated that Bishop Sergio Méndez Arceo of Cuernavaca, Mexico, was really a Jew whose job at the Council was to link the Catholic Church with Jewry and to introduce Freemasonry into the Church. It indicated that the bishop was a descendant of Spanish Sephardic Jews who once tried to Judaize the people of Cotija, Mexico. (Many Sephardim did, in fact, settle in Cotija, but the Méndez Arceo family is not from there, nor does it know of any Sephardic ancestry.)

Wild as these charges were, they were calculated to carry weight with many, both in the Council and outside. Latin Americans and southern Europeans are still emotionally fighting the ideological wars of the nineteenth century against the Freemasons, who took the lead in breaking the Church's monopoly of education in their countries. Apologetic Catholic literature, which linked Jews and Freemasons in a world-wide conspiracy to destroy the Church, is still fresh in their memories. Bishop Méndez Arceo did, in fact, urge the Council to rescind earlier condemnations of Freemasonry, but he did so within a framework of objectivity. It is true, he said, that many Freemasons are anti-Christian, but most members of that organization believe in God's revelation and are professed Christians, or at least they are engaged in no conspiracy either against the Church or against civil authority. It is a mistake, he concluded, to lump them all together as anti-Catholic.

Even today there are Catholics who believe, or at least strongly suspect, that a Jewish-Masonic conspiracy against the Church does in fact exist. This may help to explain why the vicious techniques of defamation used by the opponents of the statement on the Jews failed to cause a reaction of universal revulsion among the Fathers. Instead, the Fathers acquiesced in one postponement of discussion after another and in one modification of the text after another. While the draft moved through the Curia's mysterious channels, unauthorized and unidentified persons altered it, according to no less a witness than Cardinal Heenan of England. At the Council's third session, he declared on the floor of St. Peter's that revisions in and deletions from the document were not the work of the Secretariat for Christian Unity, the competent committee.

Specifically, Heenan charged, the unauthorized revision between December 1963 and September 1964 had dropped a phrase absolving the Jews of the charge of being deicides, or "killers of God." The retention of this phrase suddenly became a test of the honor of the Council and of the Catholic Church in the eyes of public opinion, both Catholic and non-Catholic. Bigots throughout the centuries had used the epithet of deicide as a favorite weapon. When on September 25, 1964, Cardinal Bea resubmitted the revised text, he urged the Fathers to restore the deleted phrase. Cardinal Heenan, also a member of the Secretariat for Christian Unity, supported him. He said that the text that the Fathers had in their hands was, in its present form, "not ours." Nor did he know, he added, who were the experts who had drafted it. "But let me tell you frankly, they are *periti imperiti* [inexpert experts]."

Such behind-the-scenes maneuvers to prevent the expression of majority opinion, or to thwart it when expressed, occurred many times during the Council. Even when (as on this occasion) standing orders were violated in the process, the culprits were never officially identified, still less censured. According to Xavier Rynne, the changes were made at a meeting in April 1964 of the Co-ordinating Commission, a committee through which all documents passed before distribution to the Council. René Laurentin, *peritus* and author of four important books on the Council,[1] has pinpointed the responsibility even more precisely. Statements by members of the Co-ordinating Committee,

[1] *L'Enjeu du Concile; L'Enjeu du Concile, Bilan de la première session; L'Enjeu du Concile, Bilan II; L'Enjeu du Concile, Bilan III* (Paris, Editions du Seuil, 1962–1965).

he reported, indicated that the decision was not made by the commission as a whole but by its head, Cardinal Cicognani, Secretary of State.

One thing that the Council debates confirmed was the continuing intensity of anti-Semitism among Catholics in several parts of the world. Patriarch Maximos IV Saïgh of Antioch said that "there certainly remains on the forehead of the Jewish people, as long as it is far from the Redeemer, what the prophets of the Old Testament prophesied: a stain of shame." And Bishop Luigi Carli, of Segni, Italy, was even more explicit. "I consider it legitimate to affirm that the entire Jewish people at the time of Christ was responsible collectively for deicide. . . . Judaism after the time of Christ has also, objectively, participated in the responsibility for deicide, to the extent that this Judaism constitutes the free and voluntary continuation of the Judaism of those times." For these reasons, concluded Bishop Carli, the Jews can be called "reprimanded" and "accursed of God."

While Bishop Carli attempted to justify the charge of deicide, Cardinal Ruffini of Sicily produced a different but not less specious argument for omitting the expression from the document. It is absurd for the Council to talk about deicide, he said, because it is impossible to kill God. At the same time, he revealed the depth of his own anti-Semitism by accusing the Jews of being aggressive toward the Church and of promoting anti-Catholic Freemasonry. The Cardinal's argument is specious, since it is Catholic teaching that, because of the unity of human and divine natures in Christ, whatever happened to His humanity was also attributable to His divinity. That is the basis for the Catholic belief that Mary is the Mother of God. Accordingly, to be guilty of killing Christ, the man, would indeed carry with it the guilt of deicide.

The September 1964 debate also established that opposition to the draft was confined to a small minority of bishops. The anti-Semitic arguments were overwhelmingly rejected, and the document was sent back with instructions to restore the viewpoints originally expressed by the competent commission. Here, however, a new factor came into play, one that was accorded excessive importance many times during the Council. Face-saving is a basic rule of the Roman game. The rights and wrongs, the truths or falsehoods, of the situation are secondary.

In obedience to this convention, the version resubmitted to the Council in mid-November 1964 did not absolve the Jews from deicide. It merely forbade Catholics from presenting them as guilty of deicide, leaving open the question as to whether they were or were not. Such juggling with words may have won the votes of a few prejudiced Fathers. But what did it do to the image of the Catholic Church in the eyes of honest men? Certainly the earlier comment of Cardinal Heenan remained valid. The first draft had absolved the Jews of deicide. The draft voted on and overwhelmingly approved on Friday, November 20, 1964, did not. Was it unreasonable for the world to conclude that the Fathers, on more mature reflection, had decided that they had been wrong in saying that the Jews were not guilty?

What followed was still more disturbing for world opinion and for many at the Council. Encouraged by their partial success, the opponents of the statement tried another maneuver. The Council was due to recess the day following the vote, and they persuaded the Council officials to postpone until the next session the promulgation of the document, on the ground that there was not time to get the final text printed. The supporters of the statement protested, pointing out that it did not become a Council document until promulgated. They were given the assurance that the November 20 vote had frozen the text, so that no subsequent change of any significance was possible. But who was to judge when the change of a word or two might be considered significant?

The question was answered, after a fashion, when the "modified" text (to use the technical term) emerged on September 30, 1965. It had been considerably rewritten, strengthened by several insertions, but omitted entirely the key word *deicide*. Was the omission significant? "We weren't quite sure," one who worked on this draft told the press. "We said to ourselves that we'd let the Fathers decide that point when they voted on the amendments."

In fact the Fathers were no longer free. The Council was moving toward its end, with only a few weeks to complete a still heavy schedule of work. Taking into account the long history of sidetracking, those who favored a statement decided that it was safer to accept the latest compromise than to return the draft for yet another round in committee. In consequence, the declaration as promulgated on October 28, 1965, fell far short of the forthright statement envisaged four years earlier by Pope John and Cardinal Bea. While it put the Church on record as decrying "displays of anti-Semitism," it remained cautious in the extent of rehabilitation. Specifically, the term *deicide* did not appear at any point. The document, in addition, failed to affirm that the Jews are not rejected or accursed by God. It contented itself with saying that they should not be presented as such.

An objective evaluation of these goings on must surely make clear that the Catholic Church is still a long way from the methods of the twentieth century. And when one realizes that similar manipulations of power occurred time and again during the Council to frustrate the will of the majority, one may reasonably conclude that the Council fell short of reaching the goal set for it by Pope John.

It would be a mistake, nevertheless, to leave it at that. The goal may not have been reached, but the progress toward it was phenomenal. One of the basic facts about the Council is that it established that the great majority of the bishops of the Catholic Church were responsive to the need for renewal and were ready to struggle to get it. The fact is all the more remarkable when one remembers who these men are. Under the tight centralized control of Church administration in modern times, they had been selected to be bishops because the Roman Curia decided they possessed, in addition to their orthodoxy and personal piety, such virtues as exaggerated caution, circumspection, willingness to conform, conservatism. Many were educated in Rome and there groomed to be subservient to the Curia. Many at home between Council sessions hesitated to implement the decisions for which they had voted in Rome, and complained bitterly when their people exercised the freedoms proclaimed by the Council as their Christian birthright. It is not surprising that there were conservatives as well as progressives at the Council. The miracle is that the progressives were so many and the conservatives so few.

What were the factors that influenced a given Father to vote with the conservatives or with the progressives on a particular issue? Was there much switching of sides? The most substantial study of this question was carried out by the American Jesuit Rock Caporale. At the second session he interviewed 73 cardinals and bishops from 39 nations of the 5 continents, men selected by him because their colleagues regarded them as spokesmen for significant viewpoints. Of the 73, ten had always voted with the majority, while 33 had at some time voted with the minority. The others did not clarify the point for Father Caporale.[2]

A reasonable conclusion would be that there were few totally closed minds. The Fathers tried to judge each issue on its merits. This would add to the significance of the fact that the majority was almost always overwhelmingly in one direction, namely, in the direction of the advance as outlined by Pope John. The conservative position garnered 10 per cent of the votes only on rare occasions. A greater unanimity would have raised a suspicion of rigged balloting, as it does when it occurs in political elections.

Bishop John J. Wright, of Pittsburgh, has written that his experience was less one of conservatives and progressives than one of open-minded and closed-minded people, that is to say, some who by training and attitude were ready to see two sides to a question, and others whose minds were made up and incapable of appreciating any contrary opinion. He agrees that the designations conservative and progressive also have validity, but one of less importance.[3]

The point is a good one, and it raises the question why some minds are closed. It is easy to distinguish two kinds of closed minds. Certain individuals are by temperament so totally committed to one viewpoint as not to admit the possibility of any other. Such closed minds could naturally be found in both the conservative and the progressive camps. But another and probably more important cause of closed-mindedness existed among the Council Fathers. It is the nature of the training they had received. Almost without exception they were raised in the seminaries established on the instructions of the Council of Trent. In the nineteenth century, in particular, the teaching in

[2] *Vatican II: Last of the Councils* (Baltimore, Helicon Press, 1964).
[3] "Conciliar Rome," *America*, 112 (March 27, 1965), pp. 418–420.

these seminaries reacted against the burgeoning secular culture that has led to the great scientific advances of the twentieth century. It narrowed ever further the field of free discussion, giving the students only the official side of a question. They started with an answer and were taught to develop arguments to prove that this answer was the only correct one. The result, of course, was not genuine education but indoctrination, and it is a tribute to the caliber of the men who gave themselves to the Church that so many of them rose above the system and learned as they advanced in life to give truth priority over partisanship.

Bishop Wright has further recorded that it had been his experience that other attitudes were found in both camps in about the same degree and with equal frequency, for example, the disposition to take advantage of any card that might turn up in order to win a trick.[4] A study of the record, however, shows that there was much more intrigue on the conservative side. Among the conservatives, one had the indoctrinated as well as the temperamentally closed-minded; on the other side, only the temperamentally closed-minded.

It is the indoctrinated, in fact, who formed the hard core of the opposition, and an appreciation of this reality is essential for an understanding of the conflict that occurred within the Council. These were the men who had been taught that the only community in which the Holy Spirit works is that of the Roman Catholic Church. These were the men who were taught that infallibility, as defined by the First Vatican Council, extended to every official teaching of the pope, as an encyclical addressed to all Catholics, and spilled over into the acts and decisions of the various bodies acting with the authority of the Holy See, that is to say, the curial offices. These were the men who in the Holy Office were charged with preserving the purity of the faith by banning books and silencing lecturers, men who believed that to challenge their decisions was to expose one's self to the taint of heresy and the risk of eternal damnation.

These men were trapped by their principles. They were forced to oppose all change, and in particular the kind of

[4] Ibid.

change that involved an admission that a pope, any pope, had in any circumstances been wrong. They could not concede that many of the reforms proposed by Martin Luther and other sixteenth-century Reformers were legitimate and should at this late date be accepted by Catholics. They had to insist that the modern centralization of power in Rome best met the needs of the Church and that it expressed adequately Christ's intention regarding the form His Church should take. They had to fight the concept that any who did not accept the primacy of Peter, understood literally in the terms formulated for them in their texts, could still be members of Christ's Church. They were integralists. Any breach destroyed their position entirely.

Part of the strength of the intransigent minority lay precisely in the fact that it possessed a casuistry impervious to logic. It was able to point out that the Second Vatican Council—unlike previous ones—was not called to formulate definitions. Even when it discussed matters pertaining to the faith, as in the decree on the nature of the Church, it was on record as expressing a consensus of current beliefs, not an infallible, immutable statement. The minority was accordingly able to console itself with the thought that all others were temporarily out of step, but that the truth would ultimately prevail.

What, of course, amazed everyone on the outside was that so small a number was able to achieve so much. Part of this success must be attributed to political skill. They knew how to exploit every difference within the far from homogeneous majority. Patriarch Maximos IV Saïgh, for example, was an outspoken progressive on most issues. Yet he led the opposition to the statement on the Jews, voicing the prejudices he shared with most Christians of the Near East.

More important, however, than the casual alliances on particular issues was the ability to manipulate the power structures of the Vatican, including those of the Council. To understand how these worked, it is necessary to see how the Council itself was organized.

Chapter 2

Who Writes
the Rules?

A council is an assembly called to make decisions on the Christian faith and Church discipline. If the Church of all parts of the world is represented, it is called an ecumenical, or universal, council. Otherwise, it is known as a local council. Catholics generally list as ecumenical 20 councils held before Vatican II. The first was Nicea in 325. The 19th was Trent, from 1545 to 1563; the 20th, the First Vatican Council in 1869–70. It defined the pope's primacy and infallibility.

These 20 councils exhibit a great variation in structure and composition. Bishops in charge of dioceses have always been regarded as entitled to participate, but the number and influence of non-bishops have often been substantial. Early and recent councils were primarily gatherings of bishops. The intermediate ones had a wider representation from other groups. The rise of monasticism, for example, brought abbots into prominence. The Council of Constance (1414–18) had bishops, abbots, spokesmen for ecclesiastical corporations, and doctors of theology and canon law. The corporations were of many kinds: universities, monasteries, associations or chapters formed by diocesan priests. Absent bishops were authorized to vote by proxy. And to prevent the Italians from dominating the others, voting was by "nations," each nation consisting of a grouping, or coalition, of several neighboring countries. The low point in episcopal control probably came at Basle. A vote in 1456 recorded 3 cardinals, 19 bishops, 29 abbots, and 303 "others."

Secular powers were represented at most councils and usually had the right to vote. Constantine the Great had political motives for summoning the Council of Nicea. Justinian hoped that the Second Council of Constantinople would bring Egypt back more fully into his empire by resolving the conflict over Monophysitism. All early councils were, in fact, convened by the emperor without the authorization or consent of the pope. The pope as patriarch of the West was, however, represented by legates who were given preferential treatment, even at times presiding. The representatives of the state normally presented the political policies of their respective masters, but their presence was also justified on the ground that they were the voice of the laity, and the same character was imputed to the representatives of universities. The progressive clericalization of Church structures after Trent narrowed the circle of participants. The invitation to the First Vatican Council went only to bishops and the heads of certain religious orders.

The 1917 Code of Canon Law lists those today entitled to speak and vote in a council. They are the patriarchs, the cardinals, all archbishops and bishops in charge of a diocese, plus certain abbots and heads of religious orders. Bishops not in charge of dioceses—such as assistant bishops in large dioceses, or the many members of the Roman Curia who are consecrated bishops to give them status in the Church administration—may be invited. If so, they have equal rights with the others. They were, in fact, invited to Vatican II, and at the second and subsequent sessions, the invitation was expanded to include the administrators of mission territories who were not bishops.

Those entitled to speak and vote are called Fathers. If all those summoned were to be present, they would number close to 3,000. Some, however, could not come because of illness or extreme age, others for personal reasons, or because they could not obtain exit permits or feared they might not get back if they left their countries, or because they were in jail. Nobody came from Communist China except those already in exile. The numbers from Communist countries of Europe varied with the political winds and the vagaries of the rulers, but they tended to increase as the Council progressed.

The actual number of Fathers in Rome during the sessions was always between 2,000 and 2,500. Fathers at the First Vatican Council never exceeded 700. Only 535 were present when the final vote on papal infallibility was taken. Trent usually had fewer than 100 participants, but the final session, which confirmed all the earlier decrees, had slightly over 200. Trent and previous councils could not claim to be literally representative of the Catholic world, since most of the bishops came from only a few countries. However, all decrees were approved and promulgated by the pope and accepted by the entire Catholic Church. These are the criteria theologians use to determine whether a given council is ecumenical.

Others who attended the meetings of Vatican II and made their weight felt included the *periti,* or experts in theology, canon law, liturgy, sociology, history, Scripture, and the many other subjects involved in the discussions. They numbered about 215 at the opening of the Council, and more were subsequently named. At some previous councils, the experts spoke and voted. At Vatican II, they did not vote, and spoke only at committee meetings, not in the general assembly. Most were progressives, and the conservatives who controlled procedure tried hard to downgrade them and muzzle the more outspoken, but with slight success. There were conservatives among the *periti,* too, like the "inexpert experts" whom Cardinal Heenan charged with altering the statement on the Jews without authority. Each Father could also bring a personal theologian to the meetings to act as his secretary and adviser, and many did so. Though they lacked official standing, the secretaries engaged freely in the often important discussions in the two coffee bars in St. Peter's where much of the Council business was settled.

Early in the nearly four-year period of preparation, vague but totally unrealistic hopes were expressed that Orthodox, Anglican, and perhaps even some Protestant bishops would be invited to attend as equals, speaking and voting with the other Fathers. It was unrealistic, because such an arrangement could help Church unity and Christian fellowship only if preceded by informal exchanges producing mutually acceptable ground rules. The experience of the Council of Florence could here provide a warning. It was called to heal a break between Catholics and Orthodox that had been more or less complete for several centuries. Strong feelings for reunion did exist, but were inspired more by fear of the growing strength of the Osmanli Turks than by concern for the unity wished by Christ. The upshot was an agreement based on formulas understood differently by the two sides. It achieved neither political nor religious results.

The conditions of the Protestant invitation to Trent were even less realistic. Emperor Charles V had defeated the armies of the Protestants, and he imposed as a condition for a truce that they send representatives to the Council. When Pius IX summoned the First Vatican Council in 1868, he included the various Orthodox Churches in the invitation, but again without previous consultation or without establishing an area of agreement. To make matters worse, the text had been leaked to the press before delivery to the invitees. The patriarch of Constantinople returned the pope's letter unopened, commenting that he already knew what it said. His objection, he hastened to explain, was not based simply on the breach of protocol in the premature disclosure of the text. The letter, he said, did not pay "due respect to apostolic equality and brotherhood," and consequently no benefit could be anticipated through participation of the Eastern bishops.

Pius IX's approach to the rest of the Christian world was even more indelicate. Three months after the abortive invitation to the Orthodox, he issued a public appeal "to all Protestants and non-Catholics" to return to the one fold of Christ. They reacted with understandable outrage. The Protestant High Consistory in Berlin, in a reply typical of many, rejected the letter as "an unjustified interference in our Church."

Pope John stressed from the outset that Vatican II would not be a council of unity, that is, a council to resolve differences between Christians and achieve union under a single leadership. His more modest goal was a council to prepare the way for unity. He wanted the Catholic Church to study its attitudes, teachings, and institutions that offended other Christians, and to eliminate as many of the offending elements as could be dropped without doing violence to the content of the faith and the will of Christ. "We do not intend to conduct a trial of the past," he said. "We do not want to prove who was right and who was wrong. All we want to say is: 'Let us come together, let us make an end of our divisions.' "

While recognizing the impossibility of their formal participation as members, John saw that the presence of representatives of other Christian churches would promote his objectives. It would compel the speakers to be honest and realistic in the course of the discussions. It would demonstrate the sincerity of his own assertion that "we have nothing to hide." He accordingly invited observers from all Christian Churches and communities. They would have full freedom to see and to comment on the proceedings in writing, thereby making a positive contribution, but they would not speak or vote and consequently would not commit their organizations in any way.

For reasons that will emerge later, the response from the Orthodox and other Eastern Churches was disappointing. Apart from some small groups like the Copts and the Armenians, the Council opened with representatives only of the patriarchate of Moscow, and they had arrived in circumstances that suggested a desire to steal a march on their colleagues of the other Orthodox Churches. The Churches that had grown out of the sixteenth-century Reformation, on the contrary, responded enthusiastically. Anglicans, Lutherans, Calvinists, Methodists, Baptists, and many others were represented. The 37 observers, a number that increased to almost 100 by the final session, were one of the great successes of the Council.

More disappointing for many Catholics, as well as for other Christians, was the absence of lay Catholics from the proceedings. Only one Catholic layman attended the first session— Jean Guitton, a distinguished French intellectual, invited by the pope as his guest and seated with the observers. He had no official status.

Ten laymen, officers of international Catholic organizations, were invited as "listeners" (*auditores*) to the second session. When it was later pointed out that women constituted half of all Christians but were completely absent from the Council, a token representation was added. However, the Council continued to pay little attention to women in its deliberations, this in spite of a powerful plea on their behalf from Archbishop Hallinan, of Atlanta, Georgia.

The Catholic lay delegates had neither the right to vote nor the right to speak, although a few were allowed to address the assembly on topics judged by the clerics to be of special concern to the laity. But even then they could not speak their minds freely, seldom going beyond pious platitudes. Moreover, the choice of "listeners" reflected once more the modern clericalization of the Church. Many were paid employees of the clerical establishment, their careers dependent on their ability to sail the serene waters of noncontroversy. By the final session, there were 29 laymen, 13 laywomen, and 10 nuns in the "listener" category.

Even before the Council opened in October 1962, an immense preparatory work had been undertaken, probably more than for any previous council. Commissions, offices, and secretariats were set up. Bishops were invited to forward proposals. Experts from all over the world were recruited to analyze, organize, and formulate. Nevertheless, when the Council finally began, little had been achieved, and few knew even where to begin.

Two major reasons conspired to produce this result. One was the intention of Pope John. A stultifying element in contemporary Church life was an excessive concentration of the decision process in Rome. The bishops had grown accustomed to accept unquestioningly the rulings spewed out by the offices of the Curia, which backed up its every trifling interference by invoking the authority of the sovereign pontiff. Pope John realized that the bishops would have to be made to understand that they were free and should use their freedom. A first step was for him to stay as much as possible in the background.

The other reason was that the Curia did not want a council at all, and if they had to have one, they wanted a council without substance. The pope had little choice but to use the Curia, his secretariat, to plan the Council. It controlled the preparatory bodies, and it set out to organize an agenda of such volume and complexity that, hopefully, nobody outside the Curia itself could understand. In this way, the decisions would strengthen rather than weaken its entrenched position. Meanwhile, the pope's proclaimed purposes were delicately—and sometimes not very delicately—shaded to reach an end far removed from his intention. Draft documents were loaded with denunciations and anathemas calculated to aggravate once more the relations with other Christians that Pope John was so successfully improving. The first chapter of a proposed statement on the authority of bishops, intended by those who had requested it to reassert rights ignored since Vatican I, dealt with relations between the bishops and the Curia (not between the pope and the bishops!) in terms calculated to spell out the right of the Curia to command and the duty of the bishops to obey.

A key element in the curial strategy was to control the structures of the Council itself, as it had controlled the preparatory committees. One of these was the General Secretariat, responsible for documentation, information, communications of the steering committee to the assembly, collection and transmission of written and oral suggestions of the Fathers, and drawing up texts edited by the committees. It was solidly in the curial hands of its general secretary, the relatively youthful Archbishop Pericle Felici. Felici was also secretary of the Coordinating Commission, of the presidential board known as the Praesidium, and of the Technical Commission for Organization. As a matter of routine, he saw the pope every week.

Efficient, affable, and charming, Felici had an extremely difficult job, and by universal agreement he handled the technical aspects with polish and finesse. What was less clear was his objectivity. According to Xavier Rynne, he had the interests of the minority at heart.[1] And Father Yves Congar, French theologian and pioneer of ecumenism, noted that general secretaries tend to be either generals or secretaries, with Felici more of a general. The Swiss theologian Hans Küng agreed. Reference will later be made to Felici's extraordinary outburst against newsmen in a November 1964 interview reported in *L'Osservatore Romano*.

The 10 commissions were also key structures, playing an even bigger part in the Council than do committees of the Congress of the United States in the work of that body. Each had a more or less defined area of competence: theology, liturgy, lay apostolate, the missions, and so on. They drafted the documents for debate by the Council and revised the texts in the light of the oral and written comments of the Fathers. As the Council had no machinery for the submission of amend-

[1] *The Third Session* (New York, Farrar, Straus & Giroux, 1965), p. 11.

ments from the floor, the committees had wide discretion in interpreting the wishes of speakers. Documents revised by a committee were returned to the Council for approval, and the Fathers could in theory send a document back as many times as might be necessary in order to have its wishes fully reflected in the text. But in practice a committee could incorporate many of its own ideas without risking a negative vote.

Before the Council opened, the pope had named as president of each committee the curial cardinal who had headed the corresponding preparatory committee. The Curia, as noted earlier, had picked its own men to pack the committees, but the Council rejected their lists and elected candidates who reflected more adequately the geographical and theological complexity of its members. Pope John, however, with his typical desire for conciliation, included many of the Curia's defeated candidates when he nominated 9 members to sit on each committee along with the 16 elected by the Council. The resulting body, while better than the Curia's original proposal, still fell far short of being sensitive to the moods of the Council itself. The president was usually able to put his own men in as vice-president and secretary, and among them they controlled major decisions. Pope Paul made yet another effort to narrow the gap between committees and the Council at the end of the second session, adding four elected and one nominated member to each, as well as additional vice-chairmen and secretaries. The total effect was to lessen the stranglehold of the conservatives, though not by any means to eliminate it.

One important committee managed to escape curial control —Cardinal Bea's Secretariat for Promoting Christian Unity. Begun as a preparatory secretariat, it continued with the same structure as a Council secretariat because no curial body had previously existed to perform its specific functions. First introduced as a minor body, it was later raised to full equality with the other committees. Technically, it is part of the Curia, the Vatican secretariat, but it does not share the spirit of that body. The independence of the Secretariat for Promoting Christian Unity was extremely valuable in saving the substance of the statements on the Jews and on religious freedom, both matters within its competence. However, the complicated interlocking and overlapping of responsibilities permitted other committees, as already noted, to tamper with these documents without consulting Cardinal Bea's secretariat.

The inadequate structuring of the lines of authority was one of the great defects of Vatican II. The Council was supposed to be master of its own decisions. This principle had been proclaimed time and again by both Pope John and Pope Paul. But the Council was never given organs through which it could efficiently determine its views and execute its decisions.

The original controlling body of the Council was the Presidency, a board consisting at first of 10 and later of 12 cardinals. Groups of its members presided in turn at the assemblies during the first session. At the beginning of the second session, as part of a procedural reform intended to speed up and streamline business, the job of presiding was given to a new body of four *moderatores.* The Latin word means helmsman, which is much more positive than the literal translation (moderator) generally used in English. The four moderators chosen by Pope Paul were Cardinals Lercaro, Suenens, Agagianian, and Döpfner, only one of whom (Agagianian) was a member of the Curia. However, the Presidency was continued in existence as a sort of watchdog over the order of business, and behind it was yet another board, the Tribunal of the Council, a court of appeal in questions concerning the order of business and in conflicts between the Council Fathers and the organs of the Council.

The proclaimed purpose of all this machinery was to enable the Council Fathers to formulate decisions on matters of faith and discipline. The deliberations took place at general meetings of the Fathers, normally held each morning, Monday through Friday. They started with a Mass at nine o'clock and continued until 12:30. Each text, prepared by one of the 10 committees and channeled through other committees entitled to examine its contents, came before the assembly. Any Father might express his views, make suggestions to improve the text, or urge its rejection. The rules required each speaker to submit his text ahead of time—three days at first, later five days. When the moderators judged that all viewpoints had been adequately presented, they called for a vote to cut off debate. If the majority agreed, further speakers could be heard only if they secured the signatures of a certain number of Fathers—5 at first, later 70.

Serious procedural defects were obvious from the outset. Assemblies fall into many sociological categories, the number of members playing a significant role in determining the category. Once a certain size is passed, the nature of the assembly changes. The Twelve chosen by Christ could reach unanimity after discussion. When the numbers at Church councils rose to a hundred, a more formal regime was required, but the assembly might still be classed as a community. Was this possible with 2,500, as at Vatican II, or was that assembly more like an audience or a public? The Council was conducted on the questionable assumption that it was still a community, and it retained the fiction that each of the 2,500 members had an absolute right to be heard on every question. The difficulty was not simply one of time. Technically it is impossible to co-ordinate so many viewpoints involving the substantive, cultural, and semantic differences among 2,500 individuals.

Pope John, as was noted above, left the rules deliberately vague and fluid during the first session. He wanted to stress, above all, freedom of expression, to enable the bishops to get to know one another and the many currents of opinion inside the Church. Experience would later force revision of the procedures.

If such was the pope's intention, he achieved the first part of it. To the amazement of the bishops themselves and of the whole world, it soon became apparent that a vast majority supported John's proposals for updating the Church, that they were acutely conscious of the inadequacy of many practices consecrated by modern tradition, that they clamored for decentralization and for a change of technique and spirit in the central direction of the Church, that is to say, the Curia.

The second part, however, ran into trouble. It was easy to see what procedures were inadequate. Summing up the first session, Father Congar said it suffered from two defects: the absence of a precise and reasonably restrained program, or order of the day, and the absence of a more speedy and parliamentary work method. An obvious defect, though not necessarily the most basic, was the lack of machinery to determine to what extent speeches in the assembly reflected the mind of the Fathers. Twelve speeches might cover a given point before the moderators called for a closure vote. Six might express the views of 6 Fathers; the other 6, those of 1,600 Fathers. Some speakers got around the problem in specific cases by saying that they spoke for a group of bishops or for the bishops of one or various countries. But usually it was difficult to determine whether a speaker spoke for himself or reflected the views of many.

Pope Paul introduced various changes at the start of the second session. The most radical was the already mentioned naming of the four moderators, of whom three were identified with the progressive majority. The moderators soon tried to introduce a procedure for determining the mind of the assembly. It would not only have speeded up business but, what is even more important, would have produced documents better reflecting the intentions of the Fathers. Their suggestion was not the obvious one of permitting amendments from the floor, an elementary parliamentary device but one smacking too much of democracy to be palatable to the curialists. Instead, the moderators formulated a series of questions for an assembly vote. The vote would establish the views of the Fathers on an issue on which discussion threatened to drag on forever. The issue at stake was, as we shall see, whether and in what way the bishops shared supreme authority with the pope in the Church.

The proposal brought on one of the major crises of the Council. Issues of jurisdiction and of interpretation of the rules of procedure were raised behind the scenes, revealing yet another of the peculiarities of the Council, namely, that the assembly was not master of its own procedures, in fact was not even consulted about them. After a long delay, the impasse was resolved at a meeting attended by 28 persons in the apartment of the secretary of state on October 23, 1963. Although arranged in the greatest secrecy, the meeting was reported in the *Corriere della Sera* on the following day. After a bitter discussion, in which the right of the moderators to call for orientation votes was challenged, a majority of one approved of their action. The votes were taken, and the Council went back to work.

What is even more significant, however, is the further fact that the moderators called for no more orientation votes. Here is an example of one of the subtle elements in curial politics that is difficult for those raised in other cultures to accept. One must always compromise. The moderators were allowed their Pyrrhic victory. They got their vote. But their opponents won the war. No public decision was handed down. The fact of dissension was never officially admitted.

The Council had consequently to struggle forward toward its objectives with inadequate machinery. Among the elements that were manipulated to thwart its purposes was the so-called rule of unanimity. There is, indeed, a long-standing principle governing the promulgation of Catholic doctrine, namely, that where significant difference of opinion exists, the issue is left open. The Council of Trent, at the insistence of some Venetian Fathers familiar with Greek traditions, reformulated its canon on marriage to leave a loophole for the custom of Eastern Churches, which permit divorce and remarriage in case of adultery. The unanimity rule does not, however, mean mathematically absolute agreement. What is required is a consensus so overwhelming as to reflect the entire mind of the Church. Eighteen per cent of the Fathers at Vatican I voted in the assembly against defining papal infallibility, yet the majority and the directing bodies of that Council decided that the majority in favor was big enough to satisfy the rule of unanimity. In Vatican II, the directing bodies frequently bowed to the opposition of a proportionately much smaller minority, or, as some would say, used the excuse of a small minority to impose their personal views. The justification would seem all the less valid in Vatican II, because the Council was not involved in formulating dogmatic decrees in such a way as to make them part of the Church's infallible teaching. Its work was rather to establish a series of principles that would form a coherent base for programs of action appropriate to the times.

The net effect of this experience was to intensify the previously existing bitterness between the bishops of the world and the Curia. Hans Küng summed it up with his customary incisiveness. The greatest hindrance to the progress of the Council, he wrote, was the "fundamental antagonism which has become evident in all things, an antagonism which is not so much between the majority of the Council and a minority, but between the Council and a group of the Curia, which, although small in number and without any backing from the faithful, is exceptionally powerful in that it finds itself in possession not only of the most important key positions of the Curia (Roman congregations) but also of the Council itself."[2]

The language of debate became another issue. The Curia conducts its business in Latin, and its facility with this language gave it a great advantage over bishops, few of whom could compose with precision, still fewer engage in impromptu exchange. Besides, the accents of the different countries were so far apart that a German, a Frenchman, a Spaniard, and an Englishman, to say nothing of a Texan or a Japanese, seemed to be speaking different languages. The result was that few were able to follow the speeches at the Council. Nor was there a daily verbatim report to enable the Fathers to read each afternoon what had been said that morning.

Actually, there was no objective justification whatever for using Latin. An ecumenical council is by definition an assembly of the entire Catholic Church, and Latin is not and never has been the official language of the Church. It is the official language of the Latin rite. In spite of the protests of Eastern-rite prelates, it was, nevertheless, imposed on them as part of the imperious attitude of the Curia. Only Patriarch Maximos IV Saïgh had the status and courage to ignore this prescription. He always spoke in French, and the presiding officers never dared challenge him.

Cardinal Cushing, of Boston, tried a different approach. He left the first session early, pleading that he could not understand a word. At the second, he urged a system of simultaneous translation and undertook to pay for its installation. It was announced that his proposal had been accepted and that the system would be in operation by the start of the next session, but by then the whole thing had been conveniently forgotten.

The ordinary Father who wanted to keep abreast of conciliar debates was consequently at an extreme disadvantage. After the first session, several stated publicly that they obtained a meaningful picture of the proceedings in which they had participated only when they read accounts such as those published in *The New Yorker* by Xavier Rynne, accounts criticized bitterly by the conservatives at the time as a violation of the rules of secrecy and a disservice to the Church. Later, the volume and

[2] *The Changing Church* (New York, Sheed & Ward, 1965), p. 135.

completeness of the reporting in Catholic and general dailies and periodicals grew steadily. Both in the servicing of the press and in briefings to groups of Fathers, the theology experts played an enormously important part. Their knowledge of Latin and of the ways of the Curia enabled them to fight fire with fire. They were many times reprimanded, both privately and at the assemblies by members of the directing organs, for stepping beyond their function. But in the new spirit of openness introduced by Pope John, they could and did ignore the warnings.

Many observing the Council from a distance, especially those who did not share the belief of the Fathers that the Holy Spirit was at work in their midst, guiding all these human maneuvers toward divine ends, wondered why the majority put up with so much so patiently. Many also asked why neither Pope John nor Pope Paul intervened decisively to impose the clearly determined will of the vast majority on different occasions.

The answer involves many elements. A major one is the Roman method of doing business, a tradition of diplomacy refined through a thousand years, a tradition in which all the members of the Council had been immersed to a greater or lesser extent. Even those, and they are many, who recognized that it was no longer in tune with the times, even those who had been the victims of the trickeries and deceits that form part of its practice, felt themselves obliged to respect its forms. There must not be direct challenges. There must not be a public humiliation of one entitled to the protection of protocol. It might take more time, but it is believed possible to achieve one's aims within its forms.

As far as Pope John was concerned, his already mentioned concern was to revitalize the huge reservoir of energy represented by the bishops, energy that had become progressively less used since the declaration of papal infallibility. A solution effected by him would be no solution at all. It would simply confirm the claim of the Curia that the pope constituted the only center of authority and decision in the Church. The same consideration undoubtedly weighed with Pope Paul. In addition, Paul is a man steeped in curial traditions. Even if he does not approve of all of them, he sees progress only within their forms.

What is most extraordinary is that, with all these handicaps, the Council achieved so much. The recital of facts up to now might leave the reader with the impression that nothing had changed. It would be a grievously mistaken conclusion. Pope John's vision was catalytic. To express it in terms of Catholic theology—and these were the terms he himself used when referring to the idea that struck him quite unexpectedly in January 1959—it was an inspiration of the Holy Spirit. It is also Catholic belief that the Spirit works through the human means available, using them according to their nature to effect divine purposes.

In a description of the events of Vatican II, accordingly, as of those of previous councils, the ephemeral at first glance seems to play a bigger part than the permanent. The Holy Spirit guarantees the decisions of an ecumenical council to be free from error. This does not, however, excuse council participants from the most strenuous efforts to reach the truth. Their dedication to this task will be reflected in the extent to which they distill and focus those aspects of revealed truth pertinent to the conditions of time and place that occasioned the calling of the council. That is as far as they can go. They cannot hope to express the entirety of truth in regard to the subject treated. On the contrary, the truths of religion are mysteries incapable of total comprehension by human minds or total expression in human words, so that every formulation will be partial and inadequate.

It is in this framework that one must evaluate the work of Vatican II. If it has fallen far short of a literal fulfillment of Pope John's proclaimed purpose of updating the Church to prepare the way for Christian unity and to make the Church relevant and understandable to the world of the twentieth century, it has produced changes that few thought possible 10 years earlier. Thus it restored the bishops to a meaningful partnership with the pope in the government of the Church, in the process re-evaluating the definition of papal infallibilty of the First Vatican Council in a sense far less disturbing to Orthodox and Protestants. It recognized for the layman a dignity and function he had long been denied. It broke down many of the artificial barriers that have prevented Catholics from working with other Christians and with non-Christians to promote common religious and human values.

Two kinds of questions, nevertheless, remain unanswered. Many want to know whether the changes are real and irreversible. Are they such as to guarantee that the work started by the Council will continue to a complete fulfillment of John's aims? Others ask with equal seriousness whether the changes are not excessive, whether the Council did not throw out the baby with the bathwater, losing the positive values of the Catholic Church in an effort to placate too many people holding irreconcilable positions. The following chapters will attempt to provide the material for an answer.

Chapter 3

The Bishops
Discover
Their Powers

Catholics see the Church as an institution founded by Christ. They believe that Christ named Peter the head of the Apostles, who were His principal helpers while He lived, and that He assigned to them the task of directing His work, with the guidance and help of the Holy Spirit, after He left them. They believe that the bishop of Rome, the successor of Peter, is the head of all the other bishops, who are seen as the successors of the other Apostles.

In the first centuries of the Church's life, the practical stress was on the episcopate rather than on the papacy. Rome was regarded as the first in honor, as the sign of the Church's unity, and as the final arbiter of controversies. But in practice no attempt was made to centralize the exercise of authority. Rome played a minor role in the early councils held in the East, and later councils in the West were often unsympathetic to its claims to have the final word. All through the Middle Ages, many theologians taught that an ecumenical council was above the pope.

The issue is partly semantic. Theologians today agree that an ecumenical council wields supreme authority over the universal Church. The point they clarify is that the assembly of bishops which we call a council can accomplish nothing except in co-operation with the pope, and that its decisions have no effect until approved by the pope.

Medieval theologians had a different problem. The papacy itself was split on various occasions, with two and at times three individuals claiming to be the properly elected bishop of Rome. To solve their practical difficulty, they developed the theory that an assembly of bishops representing the universal Church could determine who was the true pope, could depose a pope, and could carry out on its own authority a reform of the Church in "both its head and members," to repeat a phrase then commonly used. The opinion that a council is above the pope remained widely held for centuries. The fifteenth-century Council of Basle went so far as to constitute itself the supreme judicial and administrative authority in the Church. It chose its own officials, functioned as a court to decide lawsuits on Church matters, and granted indulgences. Similarly, the papal bull of 1520 condemning Luther's theses was not regarded by many Catholics as expressing the Church's final word. "Luther was in the Church and remains there; he can be excluded from it only if he is condemned by a judicial sentence pronounced by a general council." Such were the words in which Konrad Peutinger, of Augsburg, expressed what many believed.

The Council of Trent did, in fact, rule against Luther and the other Reformers. It said little about the relations between the pope and the bishops, but its reforms started a process that steadily built up the prestige and power of the papacy. The charges of bribery, corruption, loose living, and the sale of indulgences lost their impact as a result of changes effected by reform popes. Catholics approved and encouraged Rome's strong leadership as their best defense against the Reformers and later against the Enlightenment and the French Revolution. The theory that a council is superior to the pope gradually fell into disrepute among Catholic theologians, and opinion steadily grew in favor of a new formulation of the respective powers of pope and bishops, a definition that would spell out the pre-eminent prerogatives of the pope as the successor of Peter, the one to whom Christ had entrusted the keys of the kingdom of heaven.

This was the atmosphere in which Pope Pius IX called the First Vatican Council. It was frequently condemned at Vatican

II as triumphalist, that is, claiming that its supporters had always and everywhere acted with supreme virtue and good judgment, and attributing bad faith and malice to all its enemies. The Church of that period did not have very much to be triumphal about. But what those within its embattled walls saw most clearly was that it had survived all assaults and that it had Christ's guarantee that it would survive to the end of time. On every side they could see only enemies dedicated to their destruction. They were the forces of evil, and while individuals among them might by Christ's mercy repent of their wickedness and be granted eternal life, there was no reason to placate the organizations as such, still less to ask their help in defining and proclaiming the truth.

It was in this atmosphere that the Orthodox were invited to participate in the First Vatican Council, and Anglicans and Protestants were summoned to renounce their errors. The Council's leaders plunged into their task in the same spirit. They packed the committees to the exclusion of the minority opposed to defining papal infallibility. They discounted the objections expressed by minority spokesmen in the debates. They rejected the claim that the minority was of a size and standing to exclude "a moral unanimity" and therefore to prevent a one-sided determination of a matter still open to free discussion in the Church.

The result was a decree that first reaffirmed the primacy of the bishop of Rome as successor of St. Peter—a primacy acknowledged by most Christians though interpreted in different ways—and then added the contested clause concerning infallibility. "We teach and define," the decree read, ". . . that the Roman pontiff, when he speaks *ex cathedra*, that is, when in discharge of the office of pastor and teacher of all Christians, by virtue of his supreme apostolic authority, he defines a doctrine regarding faith or morals to be held by the universal Church, by the divine assistance promised to him in blessed Peter, he is possessed of that infallibility with which the divine Redeemer willed that His Church should be endowed for defining doctrine regarding faith and morals: and that, therefore, such definitions of the Roman pontiff are irreformable of themselves, and not from the consent of the Church."

It was never the intention of the Fathers of Vatican I to deny that the other bishops as successors of the Apostles had a special standing in the Church. On the contrary, it was planned to follow the definition of the pope's powers with another spelling out those of the bishops. However, it was mid-July when papal infallibility was finally voted. The intolerable heat of the Roman summer had arrived. The political situation in Europe had, moreover, deteriorated gravely. The session was accordingly suspended. The very next day, the Franco-Prussian War of 1870 broke out. The French withdrew their troops that had been protecting Rome. Two months later, the Italians, who had long sought to seize what remained of the Papal States and thus complete the unification of Italy, moved in. Pius IX locked himself in the Vatican, and neither he nor any successor emerged until the agreement of 1929 with Mussolini made Vatican City a sovereign state. The Council was never formally closed, but it was universally agreed that times were unpropitious for reconvening it.

Most observers today would describe as fortunate—and many Catholics would call providential—the accidental circumstances that prevented the First Vatican Council from continuing its work. In the atmosphere then prevailing, one could hardly expect a definition of the rights of bishops that would express the totality of their functions in the Church. For while there can be no theological error in a definition of Catholic teaching by an ecumenical council approved by the pope, this does not mean that the definition must express all or even the principal aspects of the truth at issue. As Hans Küng put it, one must always bear in mind the historic contingency of conciliar decrees, the thousand daily hazards that determine their concrete form, even to such details as which secretary drafted the words, or which person happened to be chairman at the discussion, or how well a speaker could express himself in Latin.[1] In a word, the Church's doctrinal declarations are always fragmentary and not exhaustive.

This crucial point was overlooked in the years following 1870. The loyalty of Catholics to "the prisoner of the Vatican" understandably urged them to a greater manifestation of their respect for the person of the pope; such a development was also en-

[1] *The Changing Church*, p. 58.

couraged by their genuine approval of the dignity and leadership of a succession of distinguished popes from Leo XIII through Pius XII. Many would look indulgently on the fact that Catholics now thronged to Rome less to worship at the tombs of the Apostles, as Christians had done from the earliest ages, than to venerate the person of the living pope. But it was a serious thing that bishops throughout the world were being made to believe they were Roman proconsuls, administrators of defined and delimited provinces, to be ruled in every detail according to directions streaming from the offices of the Roman bureaucracy, and without obligation or authority in matters involving the rest of the far-flung empire.

So far did this outlook extend that, even when Pius XII encouraged the development of national or regional associations of bishops to deal with matters of common interest, elaborate precautions were taken to retain Rome's control over their activities. When Latin America's bishops set up their own organization to deal with the pressing needs of that continent, a parallel body created in Rome in 1958 prevented the regional organization for several years from taking any independent decisions, modifying its stand only under pressure of the new forces released by Pope John.

Vatican II was not many days old when it became clear that this issue was uppermost in many minds. Among the mass of poorly organized documents prepared by the planning committees for the consideration of the Fathers, two or three were identified as getting to the core of the problems. And standing out among these was the document purporting to describe the nature of the Church, the precise issue that the First Vatican Council had planned to discuss but had never gotten around to. No question could be more basic, yet—strangely enough— the Church had been content to live its life for twenty centuries without feeling the need for a self-definition.

Previously, indeed, there had been partial formulations. The Protestants had stressed a notion of the Church as being primarily a spiritual, invisible, interior, personal concept, the major bond of union being a common faith in Christ. Against this, Catholics had emphasized the external, juridic, visible Church existing here and now on earth, clearly identified by a hierarchical order, with the pope at its summit. The Orthodox, who were not involved in the sixteenth-century conflict, avoided the two extremes. While stressing the element of communion in charity, they also recognized the hierarchy of authority of patriarch, bishops, and priests.

The constitution on the nature of the Church as submitted to Vatican II covered many elements. Its first formulation emphasized the Catholic side in the conflict with Protestantism, but the debates at the first and second sessions produced a more balanced document. First of all, they brought out a point already partly affirmed in an encyclical of Pope Pius XII, who described the Church as a body of which Christ is the head. But it also introduced metaphors to describe the mystery more dynamically as the kingdom of God on the march, as an assembly of people in whose hearts the Holy Spirit dwells, so that each receives charismatic gifts, or inspirations, to help advance the work of God in the world. We are thus presented with a tension between the spiritual and the hierarchical elements in the Church. A tension, however, is not the contradiction that some Catholic theologians conjured up in their opposition to Protestants' stress on the primacy of the spirit.

Not all the Fathers took kindly to this way of presenting the Church. Some preferred the notion of a pyramid, which had become common in Catholic apologetics. They represented all authority and spiritual wealth as flowing from the pope at the apex through the bishops and priests to the people at the base. The Council, nevertheless, took a firm stand against the pyramidal approach. Not only the pope but also the bishops, it affirmed, had been entrusted by Christ with the government of the Church. All the members had an active role, and it consequently became essential to find more precise and subtle ways of presenting the relations between the parts that constitute the Church.

The first issue was to formulate the relationship of the bishops to the pope in the hierarchy, or government, of the Church. "Many regard this as the very center of Vatican II," wrote René Laurentin shortly after the debate,[2] and most experts still agree. "The Council's deliberation on this subject," Pope Paul commented in his speech opening the third session,

[2] *L'Enjeu du Concile, Bilan de la deuxième session,* p. 40.

"will certainly be what distinguishes this solemn and historic synod in the memory of future ages."

There were many elements in the discussion, but the primary one concerned the notion of collegiality. The idea of a college comes from Roman law. It means a group of men so bound together that they have common responsibility for the operation of an institution. Vatican II proclaimed that Christ had formed such a college—the twelve Apostles—responsible for His Church, the college itself being based on a hierarchy, or series of levels of authority. In the first place came Peter with a unique commission making him the rock on which the entire visible structure was built, with the duty of confirming his brethren and of feeding the entire flock.

The Council further proclaimed that this college was and is continued by the successors of the Apostles, the pope holding the special place given to Peter as head of the college, the other bishops constituting the successors of the other Apostles and sharing their collective responsibilities. This statement means that the bishop is not a mere delegate of the pope in his own diocese, subject to arbitrary controls, but one with authority from Christ to be exercised without restrictions other than those properly determined for the common good of the Church. It means, too, that the bishops are not individuals with authority and responsibility only for the determined area of the diocese of each, but that as a body they have common responsibility for the good of the entire Church. They are a permanent community, a body that has more powers than the sum total of the powers of the individuals who form it.

Agreement was reached only after a long struggle. It involved the acceptance by the majority of some forms of wording not wholly to its liking, and also the acceptance of an "explanatory note" setting out the sense in which collegiality is to be understood. The essential teaching remained intact, but the changes strengthened the hands of those who sought to retain the curial structures unchanged and to perpetuate the existing centralized control of the entire machinery of Church organization.

The practical opposition centered around the relationship between the bishops as a "college" with rights over the universal Church and the primacy of the pope as commonly understood and presented since the definition of primacy and infallibility by Vatican I. As already indicated, this kind of thinking had deep historical roots. The medieval crises, which had the beneficial effect of gradually developing the place of Rome as the focal point of unity, also had the negative effect of distinguishing between pope and bishops to the extent of creating an opposition that objectively does not exist. As the function of the head was expanded progressively and that of the body of bishops diminished proportionately, theologians tried to justify the deformation of the body that inevitably resulted. As long ago as the Council of Trent, Diego Lainez, S.J., a papal theologian, claimed that Tradition established a distinction between the powers acquired by a bishop as a result of his reception of Orders and his powers of jurisdiction, or authority to rule his people. Later theologians carried this idea further, presenting the bishop as receiving most of his powers by a jurisdictional and revocable grant of the pope. They even forgot that those at the First Vatican Council who promoted the definition of the pope's privileges never challenged a "universal jurisdiction" in the body of the bishops. By the twentieth century, many tended to see the powers of the bishops as derived or flowing from the pope, if not simply granted by him.

What was significant about the discussion at Vatican II was that those favoring collegiality quickly convinced most of their colleagues that recent tendencies represented a misreading of true tradition. Ignatius Ziade, Maronite archbishop of Beirut, Lebanon, reminded the Council that in the early Church, bishops were not given powers, or faculties, by the pope or anyone else: they had them because of their consecration as bishops. Gradually their use of these powers had been restricted, in part because of laws made by the pope or by general councils for the good of the whole Church. This was proper, but further restrictions had crept in progressively because the bishops themselves had asked higher authority to make every trivial decision for them, thereby encouraging the proliferation of general laws about details. For example, he said, a bishop no longer had authority to read or keep a forbidden book, to say Mass outside a Church, or to permit a layman to wash various linens after their use in the celebration of Mass.

Also important was a book by Giuseppe Alberigo[3] that care-fully traced the development of the question. He pointed out, for example, that the defenders of papal prerogatives were often those who had recognized and best expressed the funda-mental tradition regarding the bishops and their collegiality. He also showed that Lainez had been wrong in asserting that the distinction between the power of Orders and the power of jurisdiction was traditional and that it was not even the ma-jority view at Trent. The net result was to develop a deep rift within the conservative minority, which usually held firmly together on issues threatening the power and importance of the Curia.

Some of the conservatives, however, did not surrender with-out a fight. Archbishop Dino Staffa, a secretary of the Con-gregation of Seminaries, continued to insist that collegiality was unhistorical and injurious to the pope's rights and pre-rogatives as defined at Vatican I, ignoring the fact that many strong supporters of papal infallibility at that Council never challenged collegiality as a principle. He headed a group that circulated pamphlets to the Fathers, organized lectures, and lobbied in other ways.

Archbishop Pietro Parente, as assessor of the Holy Office, on the contrary, was won over to collegiality so completely that he was chosen as majority spokesman for a final summing up before voting. His statement, in which he referred to Alberigo's book, made a deep impression. The September 1964 vote on articles 19 and 20 of the decree—the two dealing concretely with the collegiality issue—found 2,103 Fathers in favor and only 106 against.

The discussions and maneuvers that led to this consensus and the approval of a conciliar text are very interesting. They clarify the way the Council operated, the forces at play, the problems of procedure, and the benefits to be obtained by a last stand even after it is clear beyond doubt that one side has won and the other lost.

From October 4 to October 15, 1963, the Fathers debated the third chapter of the draft decree on the nature of the Church, the chapter describing the Church's hierarchical structure, and

[3] *Lo sviluppo della dottrina sui poteri nella Chiesa universale* (Rome, Herder, 1964).

specifically the role and place of the bishops in that structure. The debate centered on five issues: the nature, or character, of the bishop's consecration, that is to say, the way in which he is different from an ordained priest; collegiality; the relation of the bishop and of the college of bishops to the pope; the diaconate; the priesthood.

Catholics believe that ordination gives a priest certain powers that distinguish him from a layman—for example, the power to celebrate the Mass and, in certain defined circumstances, the power to forgive sins. They think of a bishop as a priest who receives additional powers from his consecration—for example, the power to ordain priests and to consecrate other bishops.

Theologians and historians, however, tend to be less precise. There have been definite instances of laymen and deacons who were consecrated bishops without having first been ordained priests, and theologians have always agreed that the consecration gave both the powers of the priest and the additional powers of the episcopate. More complicated is the case of the medieval English abbots who were not bishops and yet were authorized to ordain priests, which suggested that a priest could ordain another priest. And St. Jerome in the sixth century reported that in Alexandria a group, or college, of priests for a time ordained their own bishop. Was any real difference left between the bishop and the priest? Some theologians of the Western Church, steeped in Rome's legal attitudes, came up with a casuistic solution. The entirety of the sacrament of Orders is conferred by the ordination of the priest, they theorized, but it takes episcopal consecration to permit the priest to exercise certain of the powers he enjoys. Or as the Council wags put it, "a priest is a bishop with his hands tied, and a bishop is a priest with his hands untied."

Such was the first issue. As the debate progressed, it seemed clear that agreement was possible on certain basic points. Christ had not established the orders of bishop, priest, and deacon in the specific form in which we know them. He had chosen the Twelve and given them the priestly powers to be perpetuated in the Church. The episcopate is the sacrament of apostolic succession. It identifies those charged with continuing the work entrusted by Christ to the Twelve. The priest and the deacon evolved gradually as helpers of the bishop, ordained by the bishop to perform certain parts of his work but not joining him in the group charged with the total task of carrying forward the work of the Twelve. The conclusion was that an essential and distinguishing effect of consecration is to make the bishop a member of the group, or college, of the successors of the Apostles. The notion of collegiality is thus tied directly to that of episcopal consecration.

It all seems perfectly logical, argued the opposition, but it leaves one essential question unanswered. How can the collegiality of the bishops be reconciled with the primacy of the pope as defined at Vatican I? When it finally emerged after much discussion, the answer was very simple. The authority of the pope and that of the bishops to rule the Church are not two separate, possibly conflicting, authorities. They are one and the same authority, because the pope is a part, an absolutely essential part, of the college of bishops. He is its head. That is why he has the primacy, or first place, in the Church. When he solemnly proclaims a doctrine regarding faith or morals to be held by the universal Church, he speaks infallibly because he speaks as the head of the college of bishops. The way in which a pope might exercise this function as head of the college cannot be spelled out completely because it is bound to evolve according to circumstances. It is nevertheless noteworthy that the pope has exercised it on only two occasions—for the definition of the Immaculate Conception in 1854 (before his own infallibility was defined by Vatican I) and for the definition of the Assumption of the Virgin Mary in 1950—and that on both occasions he used exhaustive methods of consultation with the bishops of the world to ascertain that both the bishops and the whole body of the faithful approved before he made his proclamation.

What is also clear is that if the pope is head and the bishops are the body of the college, then a true conflict cannot arise. A body without its head can no more act than can a head without its body. The pope's infallibility is not personal. It is, as Vatican I defined, "that infallibility with which the divine Redeemer willed that His Church should be endowed for defining doctrine." If he resigns from the papacy, as he can and as popes have done, he ceases to enjoy it, because he ceases to be head of the college of bishops. Equally, if a bishop or a group of bishops cut themselves off from the head of their college and make independent decisions, as happened for a time at the Council of Basle, they cease by this act to be part of the college of bishops.

At this point the rational argument seemed to have been exhausted. No objective conflict between the notion of the primacy of the pope and the collegiality of the bishops remained. But traditions, prejudices, habits of mind, and vested interests were not therefore erased. All of these in a more or less conscious way still influenced a small group of the Council Fathers, and they continued to oppose the declaration, or sought at least to weaken it. If we agree that the bishops as a body have authority over the whole Church, they insisted, we must then concede that bishops have the right to take part in the government of the Church, and that would limit the supreme power of the pope.

The problem is that such people conceive of the Church in terms applicable only to the state. The Church, however, is a living organism in which each part helps the functioning of the other. Far from limiting the pope as head by performing their proper functions in the body, the bishops enable him to perform his function better and more normally. If a man is paralyzed or bound, his head may be able to keep him alive and may possibly restore the functions of the body, but it is perfectly obvious that his health is better when all his organs are free to work properly.

A second defect of this approach is that it distorts the nature of the Church by putting the legal relationships out of perspective. Christ chose the Apostles less to rule the people than to serve them. They rule only insofar as ruling is necessary as part of their service of love. The pope is not an arbitrary ruler, nor is the bishop. They are bound by the intention of Christ: "You know that those who are regarded as rulers among the Gentiles lord it over them, and their great men exercise authority over them," He told His Apostles. "But it is not so among you. On the contrary, whoever wishes to become great shall be your servant; and whoever wishes to be first among you shall be the slave of all; for the Son of Man also has not come to be served but to serve, and to give his life as a ransom for many" (Mk 10:42–45).

Long after everything worth saying on both sides had been said, the opposition dragged out the debate. But it gradually became clear that the filibuster could not last forever. On October 15, 1963, the Fathers agreed almost unanimously to return the text to committee to be redrafted in the light of the debate.

While the Council moved on to the next item on its program —the section of the same decree concerning the place of the laity in the Church—the opponents of collegiality continued the battle behind the scenes. The issue on which they seized was a procedural one. The speeches and written observations had revealed a wide range of positions on a series of controverted questions, and the redrafting committee insisted that it could not undertake its work until it had some idea of the majority view on each major question.

It was at this point that the moderators hit on the expedient, referred to in the previous chapter, of an orientation vote. In fact, Cardinal Suenens, presiding moderator of the day, told the Council on October 15 that such a vote would be held two days later but that the wording of the questions was not yet fully worked out. What he did not say, although many already suspected it, was that the moderators were involved in a full-scale battle with the other Council organs on the issue. That battle was, of course, being conducted in terms of the usual conventions of curial-dominated Church diplomacy. At stake was something far more basic than the concrete issue, namely, control of the Council.

On October 16, the secretary general announced that the vote proposed for the following day had been cancelled. The assembly's reaction was significantly negative. Many feared that Pope John's reform program was dead, that finally the progressive majority was face to face with the power of the entrenched civil service, and that it lacked the means to impose its will. For two weeks the Council continued its work in a dream world, discussing the chapter on the laity until October 25, then the chapter on holiness in the Church.

Behind the scenes, the conflict raged. On October 17, Cardinal Ottaviani, head of the Holy Office and leader of the conservatives, saw the pope. So did the moderators, at a later hour. On October 21, Cardinal Suenens saw the pope. On October 23, as mentioned earlier, 28 people met secretly in the apartment of the secretary of state. They comprised the entire leadership of the Council, all the members of the Presidency (except Cardinal Tappouni), the Co-ordinating Committee, the moderators, and the secretary general. Also present was Ireland's Cardinal Browne, the former head of the Dominican Order who shared Cardinal Ottaviani's reputation for intransigent conservatism, and who had been responsible for drafting the document at issue. Various issues were discussed, but the basic one was the right of the moderators to submit orientation votes to the assembly. The conservatives saw clearly that acceptance of this principle would transfer control of procedure to the other side. Finally, a compromise was reached, though by only one vote. The moderators could save face by having their way this one time. On October 29, the text of five questions was distributed and the Fathers voted the following day.

The first question asked if episcopal consecration constituted the highest degree of the sacrament of Orders, and the affirmative answer exceeded 98 per cent of the votes. The Fathers were next asked if consecration made a bishop, in union with the other bishops and the pope, a member of an episcopal body with the pope as its head. Again the affirmative answer was overwhelming, 97.6 per cent. The third question raised a new issue. For the first time the word *college* was introduced. In ancient Roman law, the word had a technical meaning. All members of a college had equal rights. Even if they chose a chairman, they could overrule him. To interpret the collegiality of the bishops in this sense would clearly overthrow the primacy of the pope as defined at Vatican I. The question, however, was phrased to meet this objection. Is the body, or college, of bishops the successor of the college of Apostles, and does it in consequence enjoy, in communion with the pope as its head, full and supreme power in the universal Church?

It was a big step beyond the previous question, and it was intended to throw a light on the definition of the pope's primacy and infallibility very different from that which had been popular since Vatican I. Quite a few Fathers were not ready to go so far, but the majority was still impressive, 1,808 votes for and 336 against, a majority of 84.3 per cent.

The fourth question was more technical but an important one. Did this supreme power over the Church belong to the bishops in union with the pope by divine right, or did it flow from a Church decision that might at some time be reversed? Was it, in a word, a concession by the pope that a future pope might similarly withdraw? Some of the negative votes were perhaps dictated more by a sense of reverence for the pope than by any serious theological concern. Affirmative answers to the first three questions seemed to call for an affirmative answer to this one. The negative votes, nevertheless, were more numerous than before, 408 out of a total of 2,125. That still left more than 80 per cent affirmative, well over the two-thirds needed for an irreversible Council decision.

The war seemed won. What seemed most decisive to many observers was that Pope Paul was clearly with the majority. In the collegiality of the bishops, he saw no challenge to his own prerogatives as pope. He had said so in his address at the opening of the session: "You are apostles, you have your origin in the college of the Apostles, and you are their true heirs." It was also well understood that he still approved the notion of collegiality, although he had followed the good precedent set by Pope John and avoided taking sides in Council issues.

But matters are never that simple in Rome. For one thing, the moderators, apparently bound by a gentlemen's agreement, never again proposed an orientation vote, though the need for one arose many times. Their attempt to improve the utterly inadequate working procedures of the Council had failed. Conservatives in key behind-the-scenes positions retained the power to manipulate the Council and obstruct the will of the majority.

In addition, the discussion of the remaining chapters of the decree on the nature of the Church was not completed until the following year, so that a final vote was delayed until November 1964. In early November, the rumor machine was once more in full production. The redrafting of the text was in the hands of the Theological Commission. Cardinal Ottaviani, head of the Holy Office, was its president, and Cardinal Browne its vice-president. While the rules of procedure permitted only modifications of detail, the heads of the committee enjoyed considerable discretion in determining what was detail and what substance. All the rumors agreed that collegiality was delaying the distribution of a final text. Many suspected that the Fathers would finally be presented with a version so watered down as to be unacceptable. All they could do would be to reject it and hopefully have the opportunity to start afresh a year later.

Fortunately, the issue was not presented quite so brutally, though indeed it was harsh enough. On Saturday, November 14, the Fathers were handed a revised text on collegiality to be voted on the following Thursday. There was no substantial change, but it was preceded by an "explanatory note." Before the vote, the secretary general of the Council told the Fathers that the explanatory note was normative, that is to say, a binding interpretation of the meaning of the text, and that it "formed part of the official acts of the Council."

The authorship of the note was never officially acknowledged. The Fathers were simply told that it was from "higher authority." Archbishop Parente, the assessor of the Holy Office who had defended the text in the assembly a year earlier, said, however, in *L'Avvenire d'Italia* that Pope Paul, in order to meet the conscientious objections of some who were doubtful about the proposed statement on collegiality, had asked the Theological Commission to prepare the explanatory note.

The main points of this extremely technical note are as follows: The term "college" is not to be understood in the strict sense of Roman law but in a special sense as a body acting with, yet always subordinated to, its head. While the bishop receives powers to teach, sanctify, and govern by his consecration, he is entitled to use them only while a member of the college (which, of course, involves association with its head). The college is described as enjoying full and supreme power in the Church only insofar as the pope is part of it, and not otherwise. The pope alone can exercise this supreme power. And if the bishops act independently of the pope, they are not acting as a college and consequently cannot exercise full and supreme authority.

Does the explanatory note limit in any way the proclamation of collegiality in the conciliar document? Those who had opposed the text itself evidently thought it did, for in the final November 19 vote, 2,134 Fathers approved and only 10 opposed. Some of the 10 may even have been Fathers who supported the text but wanted to protest the addition of the explanatory note. Indeed, at the time the incidents occurred, many spokesmen of the majority expressed bitter disappointment at having been maneuvered into taking something much less than they had demanded. Xavier Rynne, for example, complained that collegiality, as the bishops had hoped to get it, envisioned a constant harmony and identification of thought and action between the pope and the bishops. Instead, he said, they got an image of unresolved and at times conflicting dual headship, the image underlined by the explanatory note with its concern for asserting at all costs the pope's independence of action, which the bishops had never questioned.[4]

Archbishop Parente of the Holy Office, who was head of the subcommittee responsible for the text of this chapter, took a different view. The explanatory note, he wrote in a newspaper article, added nothing substantial. All the doctrinal points it contained were already in the text.[5] René Laurentin agreed with him, while regretting the addition of the note. What it did, he said, was to underline the points that the text glossed over.[6] The failure to take a forthright stand on these points did not detract from the basic value of what had been done, but it made a bad impression on those outside the Church who had hoped for more, especially the Orthodox.

The Fathers who sought a clear formulation of collegiality did so primarily because they believed that this was the way Christ meant the Church to function. In consequence, as soon as the principle was accepted, they began to urge that other decrees should be so worded as to reflect the principle, thereby starting a reform of Church structures to give the bishops a bigger voice in decisions.

The decree on the duties of bishops promulgated at the final session projects collegiality into the area of national and regional conferences of bishops. It praises those countries that (like the United States) have already formed a conference of bishops and urges that bishops everywhere belonging to the

[4] *The Third Session*, p. 4.
[5] *L'Avvenire d'Italia* (January 21, 1965).
[6] *L'Enjeu du Concile, Bilan de la troisième session*, p. 260.

same nation or region form an association to meet at fixed times. Whereas, in the past, the decisions of such conferences were only advisory, the decree provides for binding decisions by a two-thirds majority. The anticipated effect of this provision is that there will be more uniformity of application of the Council's decisions within a given country or region. An individual bishop, for example, will no longer be able to drag his feet in implementing the new liturgy. It is also anticipated that when the new conferences get moving, they will assume many of the functions hitherto exercised by the Curia, effecting a significant decentralization of Church decisions.

The decree on the Church's mission activity also leans heavily on the principle of collegiality. The entire Church, it asserts, is responsible for the needs of the entire Church, and the body of bishops "is responsible for the preaching of the Gospel everywhere." The episcopal conferences of countries that are relatively well supplied with priests and material goods are instructed to make arrangements for sharing them with areas in which the need is greater.

On a still higher level, the bishops began to ask how they could continue, after the Council, to co-operate directly with the pope in serving the Church. The various suggestions quickly coalesced into a proposal for a senate of representative bishops. It would meet frequently in Rome or elsewhere and serve as a body to discuss policy and reflect the viewpoints of the world's different geographical and cultural regions. Those who spoke of a "senate" were not thinking of a body like that of the United States, which wields immense authority. Their sights were set on something more modest, like England's House of Lords or the Senate of Ireland and various countries of Europe. These bodies are primarily consultative and advisory, but they are respected. Their wishes cannot ordinarily be ignored.

Pope Paul's speech at the closing of the Council's third session in November 1964 indicated that he intended to create such a body. Much, nevertheless, depended on the way in which he implemented his decision. Would it be a body hand-picked by Rome, the members named for life? In that case, it would in all likelihood be unable to retain for long its independence of the Curia. Instead, it would likely be drawn into the Curia's orbit or even become a part of it.

Disappointment was great, consequently, when in early 1965 Pope Paul announced an expansion of the college of cardinals. Intended to give greater representation to the non-Italian world, the move was interpreted as his way of implementing his promise, but it had the disadvantages just mentioned. Cardinals are named by the pope, are almost invariably old men when named, and continue in their functions for life. There was yet a further inconvenience. Technically, a cardinal is an official of the diocese of Rome. He is only indirectly associated with the work of the pope as pastor of the universal Church.

So the matter stood, at least publicly, until the opening of the Council's final session in September 1965. In his opening address, Pope Paul provided a dramatic surprise. In accordance with the wishes of the Council, he said, he proposed to set up an episcopal synod "composed of bishops to be chosen for the greater part by episcopal conferences and approved by us," to be convened for consultation and collaboration "when for the general good of the Church this will seem opportune to us." The very next day, with a speed unusual in Rome, the pope appeared in St. Peter's to present in person his formal plan of implementation.

The document (*Motu Proprio*) contained much to please the bishops and nothing to suggest a hesitation or drawing back by Pope Paul, as many had feared. Substantial representation is given to the various rites other than the Latin rite. For the Latin rite, bishops are to be elected by national or regional conferences of bishops. There will be 1 representative for conferences having 25 or fewer members; 2 for conferences with 26 to 50 members; 3 for conferences with 51 to 100 members; and 4 for those which—like the United States and Italy—have more than 100 members. Religious orders in the Church will also be represented by 10 members elected by the heads of the orders. Cardinals of the Roman Curia are also members, and the pope may name additional bishops or experts, but never to exceed 15 per cent of the basic membership. This ensures that a substantial majority will always be non-curial.

The pope determines the time and place of meetings and

decides the subjects to be discussed. This could, in strict legal theory, negative everything, but the weight of public opinion has become such that not even a pope could propose so specific a scheme unless he really intended to implement it. The situation seems to parallel the evolution of the British constitutional system. Like the pope, the king of England is in legal theory absolutely sovereign. Decision in fact rests with his elected ministers, but what they do is done in his name and on his authority. In Rome, a similar evolution began a long time ago, except that it represented a transfer of power to the permanent civil service, the Curia. What is now envisaged is the substitution of the synod of bishops.

Finally, new elections will be held for each session of the synod. This avoids the danger of a preponderance of old men no longer able to function. The problem of old men in authority is a real one in the Church. Many bishops urged a compulsory retirement age for themselves, but on that proposal they never got anywhere.

Agreement on the principle of collegiality, with the start of its practical application in the elected synod of bishops, is generally agreed to be the keystone of the work of Vatican II. Not all projections were carried through to their conclusions. As Hans Küng has said, some will deplore the Council's failure to see that collegiality is not merely a characteristic of the relationship of the pope and the bishops but a characteristic of the Church as such, to be projected into bishop-priest and priest-people relations.[7] Seemingly irreversible forces have, nevertheless, been set in motion, and one can anticipate the gradual translation into practice of the logic of the principles. The era of the papacy as an absolute, even arbitrary, monarchy is ended. The deformation, begun at Vatican I and compounded by subsequent legalistic theologians, has been corrected. The hierarchy in the Church is once more being seen and seeing itself as a dedication to service, the means established by Christ for performing certain of the functions of the whole people of God.

To reach this conclusion, however, the Council had to ask itself just what exactly is the people of God and what are its

[7] *The Changing Church*, p. 132.

duties and functions as such. The notion had once been clear, but centuries of development had covered it with the cobwebs of misunderstanding and prejudices. Again, the Council faced up to its task and came up with a reasonably satisfactory conclusion.

Chapter 4

The Layman
Finds His Place

Collegiality, according to Hans Küng, is a characteristic of the Church as the community of the faithful. Not only is the collegiality of the pope with the bishops to be taken seriously, but also that of the bishops with pastors and that of the pastor with the people of his parish.

The Council did not spell out all these implications of its statement on collegiality. But it did throw significant light on one element. God, it said, "does not make men holy and save them merely as individuals, without bond or link between one another." Rather, those who believe in Christ are called to form "a people made up of Jew and Gentile . . . the new people of God." Starting from this concept, the Council was able to present a better understanding of the activity that is proper to all members of the Church. This is, after collegiality and, indeed, as a part of it, one of the great perspectives opened up by Vatican II. Its study of the notion of the people of God logically carried the Council to a re-evaluation of clerical-lay relations. It also guided it in formulating the Church's fresh approach to the world, which was one of the major tasks entrusted to it.

The expanded role envisaged by Vatican II for the laity results ultimately from a new awareness of Church tradition. This is a point on which the so-called progressives of Vatican II were most emphatic. Far from beginning as though theology had become a science when they started to study it, they chided their opponents—who called themselves traditionalists—with confusing Tradition and current opinion. What had to be asked at each moment, the progressives insisted, was what Christ had intended. In this particular instance, what did the practice of the early Church reveal as the relationship that Christ established among the members of His Church?

In addition to the theological reason for clarifying the roles of clergy and laity, practical (or, in technical terminology, pastoral) reasons also demanded it. Modern practice had reduced the participation of the laity in the liturgy to little more than a passive presence. The sixteenth-century Reformation had challenged important aspects of Catholic teaching on the Mass and the sacraments. The Church's reaction was to insist that these rituals, by virtue of Christ's determination, conferred grace on one with the right dispositions, even if the individual was only marginally involved. Theologians continued to make fine distinctions, but in practice what was stressed as important was to be physically present at Sunday Mass, because the priest said it was a mortal sin not to be there. This emphasis was strengthened when some of the Reformers began to assert that all the faithful were equally priests. Theologians continued to admit that all the baptized participate in a common priesthood, but what they stressed was the special priesthood of the ordained cleric.

The practical disadvantage of this arrangement was that in many countries the laity got tired of standing in the back of the Church, without any purpose they could grasp, while a priest in exotic costume and with his back to them went through unintelligible rites for half an hour on Sunday morning. They simply stopped going to Mass. In nominally Catholic countries like France and Italy, not one adult in ten goes regularly to Mass on Sundays. Elsewhere, as in Latin America, the rites became regarded by many as essentially magical, to be combined with the other magic rites handed down from indigenous and African ancestors.

In the early Church, there was no such distinction between laity and hierarchy. The Church was the people of God, in Greek, *laos*, from which comes the English word *laity*. Originally, the Church consisted—in the sense in which its members understood the word—only of the laity. Some of the laity were called to special service: to say Mass, administer certain sacraments, preside at assemblies that decided on common action, and carry out the decisions of the assembled *laos*. Such local assemblies elected bishops and even the pope. Baptism made one a full and authority-bearing member of the Church. The appropriate degree of the sacrament of Orders— the diaconate, the priesthood, or the episcopate—distinguished those called to special service.

Many blame the Middle Ages for the change. It is un-doubtedly true that the change became fully effective then. In the times of the early Church Fathers, the whole people still participated actively in the prayer of the Church. Baptism was not easily conferred on an adult. He had to prove himself by a long period of test and preparation as a catechumen.

Nevertheless, the ideas that sprouted in the Middle Ages had probably been planted much earlier. The early Church con-sisted of poor, simple, and poorly educated men. What formal education did most of the Apostles have? There were ad-mittedly cultured Christians from an early date, as is obvious to anyone who reads St. Paul's letters. But the mass of the faithful were poor Jews and the poor of other races, the slaves of Rome, for example. While this situation lasted, all were equal in char-ity in the Church, huddling together to strengthen one another's faith and courage.

In due course, however, Christianity became popular. Con-stantine made it the state religion, and it became a force in civil life. It soon became necessary to build a bridge between the Semitic culture of the founders and the very different cul-tures of Greece and Rome. Plato was Christianized by St. Augustine, as Aristotle would later be by St. Thomas Aquinas. But over and above that, the entire Greek and Roman way of life was made the vehicle, the historical culture, in which most of the Church dressed and presented itself.

One of the basic elements of this culture was the class struc-ture. Plato and Aristotle found no difficulty in envisaging a society in which most people would exist at a primitive material, intellectual, and spiritual level in order to provide the good life for a chosen few and accord them the leisure to be philoso-phers. They regarded this division of function as a law of nature, part of what Catholic philosophers would later call the natural law. The same idea caused even less searching of conscience for the Romans, never as highly civilized as the Greeks. Nor was their attitude totally unreasonable for the time. Technology had evolved only to a level capable of giving a high standard of living to a tiny proportion of the members of any given society. To go further, they had to do what the Communists have done in our day, namely, sacrifice the mass in order to accumulate material and cultural capital.

This is where the class structure infiltrated the Church along with Greek philosophy and Roman power. It has not yet died out, although in our Western civilization the modern progress of technology has enabled us to produce a gross national product adequate to permit all citizens to live humanly. One sees the class structure in Italy and Spain, as well as in the time-lag countries of Latin America, like Colombia and Peru, where those who belong have rights and the rest merely have duties. And it is important to understand that it can persist indefinitely if there is no true awareness of human equality.

Roman Catholicism's unwillingness in modern times to accommodate to the advances of secular culture meant that it lagged behind civil society in rejecting class privileges. The sociological tension in the more advanced countries had become so acute as to force certain tactical adjustments. Lip service was paid to the importance of the laity. Certain narrow areas of competence were identified in which they might function as auxiliaries of the clergy and in specific subordination to them. But few clerics were willing to regard the layman as an adult and to recognize that he had an immediate right and duty to participate in Christ's work simply because he was a Christian.

What was sought at the Council was a revindication of the *laos* as in truth constituting the Church—not a revolt of the laity against the clergy but a new and fuller communion between both elements. And while sociological factors encouraged the re-evaluation, they were not the objective reason for it. That was, as the Council declared, the fact that such was God's scheme in creating and saving the world. He "does not make men holy and save them merely as individuals, without bond or link between one another." Rather, He first chose the Jewish race in His covenant with Moses, then in a new covenant expanded His promise to include both Jews and Gentiles, all those who have Christ as their head. "The state of this people is that of the dignity and freedom of the sons of God, in whose hearts the Holy Spirit dwells as in His temple. Its law is the new commandment to love as Christ loved us."

The decree insists, as Catholics always believed, that there is an essential difference between the common priesthood of the laity and the special priesthood of those ordained to be ministers, or servants, of the people of God. Only the ministerial priest "acting in the person of Christ, makes present the Eucharistic sacrifice, and offers it to God in the name of all the people." But the decree equally insists on the priesthood of the people, their right and duty to participate actively in the same service to God. "The faithful, in virtue of their royal priesthood, join in the offering of the Eucharist. They likewise exercise that priesthood in receiving the sacraments, in prayer and thanksgiving, in the witness of a holy life, and by self-denial and active charity." All are called by Christ not only to bear witness by their life but also to "give an answer to those who seek an account of that hope of eternal life" which they enjoy.

Another fundamental aspect of the Church brought out in the decree is the presence and function of charisms in its daily life. It is not only through the sacraments and the ministries that the Holy Spirit sanctifies and leads the people of God and enriches it, says the decree, but also by distributing "special graces according as he wills" (1 Cor 12:11).

This idea of everyone having an initiative, of being able to use his own judgment and make his own contribution to the building up of the kingdom of God, was anathema to the legalistic theologians of the later Middle Ages. To admit such a principle, they felt, would lead to anarchy and would destroy the Church as an institution. When the Reformers, by way of reaction, insisted on the primacy of private judgment in religious matters, such theologians were confirmed in their view. Many went so far as to say that charisms were something granted only to the infant Church because of its special needs, that they died out either with the Apostles or shortly afterward. Others continued to admit the theoretical possibility of charisms but in practice insisted that express approval of the hierarchical

Church was required before undertaking any external spiritual work.

Cardinal Suenens of Belgium, in a speech at the Council, gave a fine summary of what charisms are and what part they play in the life of the Church. Far from being peripheral and unessential phenomena, he said, they are of vital importance. Throughout the centuries, from the foundation of the Church until the second coming of Christ, when all things will be fulfilled, we live in the time of the Holy Spirit, and the Holy Spirit "is not given to pastors only but to each and every Christian" by Baptism. The Holy Spirit shows himself in the great number and richness of His spiritual gifts, the charisms, a subject on which St. Paul wrote frequently and in much detail. To St. Paul, the Church "did not appear as some kind of administrative organization but as a living web of gifts, of charisms, of services." The nature of these varies according to the need, the need being always to build up the Church. But every Christian, "whether lettered or unlettered," has his charism, his inspiration from the Holy Spirit to play an active part in building up the kingdom of God.

Nor are the higher charisms necessarily given to those enjoying the higher positions in the hierarchy. "The Spirit breathes where he wills," as Scripture tells us. "What would our Church be like," Cardinal Suenens asked, "without the charisms of prophets, that is, men speaking under the inspiration of the Holy Spirit, who, speaking out insistently 'on all occasions, convenient and inconvenient,' woke up the Church at times when it was asleep?" St. Francis of Assisi was a layman when he founded the Franciscans. He never became a priest, still less a bishop. St. Ignatius of Loyola was a wounded soldier in a hospital when he made the decision that led to the founding of the Jesuits.

And so on down to the more commonplace charisms that one can see daily in every area of Christian activity. "It is the duty of pastors to listen carefully and with an open heart to laymen," the cardinal continued, "and repeatedly to engage in a living dialogue with them. For each and every layman has been given his own gifts and charisms, and more often than not has greater experience than the clergy in daily life in the world."

The specific words of Cardinal Suenens are not inserted in

the decree, which treats charisms only briefly, but it does contain the principles he developed. It is easy to see that as this new—or rather restored—concept of relationships within the Church percolates downward and becomes understood by the Catholic communities of the world, both clerical and lay, the institutions and practices of the recent past must change radically.

Some of the institutional changes were indicated by the Council itself in various documents. Speaking of the Roman Curia, for example, the decree on bishops said that "it would be most advantageous if these same departments would listen more attentively to laymen who are outstanding for their virtue, knowledge, and experience." The same decree envisaged a similar role for laymen in the diocesan structures. "It is greatly desired," it said, "that in each diocese a pastoral commission will be established over which the diocesan bishop himself will preside and in which specially chosen clergy, religious, and lay people will participate. The duty of this commission will be to investigate and weigh pastoral undertakings and to formulate practical conclusions regarding them."

The Council did not content itself with calling for more active participation of the laity within the institutions of the Church. It was even more emphatic, in the decree on the laity, on the need for self-initiated action by the laity outside and beyond the Church's institutions, and specifically in the area of the daily work of each. This decree demolished the idea that the layman's only duty is to think of the world in terms of his own salvation, being explicit about his duties to the nation and to the international community. For such action, it said, the layman does not have to wait for a specific mandate from his bishop, because his duty to engage in it flows directly from his membership in the Church through Baptism and Confirmation. One can anticipate a significant change in the extent and even in the nature of Catholic participation in community work as the ideas developed by the Council infiltrate into Catholic education and permeate the culture and value systems of Catholics. They will reply less on external pressure groups seeking to influence political, economic, educational, or other decisions from a sectarian viewpoint. Instead, they will participate as mature individuals in a community process which they recognize as important in itself and to be judged by its own intrinsic values.

As this process of integration of the Catholic laity into the institutional life of the Church and into the total life of the community progresses, the whole legalistic distinction of the people of God into clergy and laity will have to be rethought. What is a layman? Canon law, in one of its less inspired moments, skipped over the issue by saying that a layman is one who is not a cleric. Several of the Fathers urged the Council to provide a more positive definition. Perhaps it was wise not to make the attempt. The Church is not yet ready to face this issue in its entirety, just as it was not ready at Vatican I to face the issue of collegiality, which fructified in a substantially satisfactory way at Vatican II. John Cogley's comments on the attitudes he encountered at Vatican II are pertinent. Cogley, who reported on the Council for various American publications, said that "as a layman, you are on the outside looking in." In spite of much talk about the layman's role, "he is more of a Hollywood extra than a supporting actor." In the mind of the clergy who ran the Council, he added, there was a greater distance between a cleric and a layman than between a Catholic and a non-Catholic. "The Protestant clergyman is more 'in' in Rome than the Catholic layman." As for the handful of Catholic lay auditors, he dismissed their presence as so much window dressing.[1]

Notwithstanding this clerical bias, the Council improved the status of the laity significantly. It dismissed the argument that recognition of charisms would produce anarchy by recalling the scriptural teaching that charismatic freedom of action is not contradictory to hierarchical authority, that, in fact, the bishops have a special gift, or charism, from the Spirit, by virtue of which they have authority to regulate the use of charisms by others. How is this done? In the most advanced civil societies known to man, the same tension between authority and freedom always remains, but a working compromise results from conventions enforced less by sanctions than by public opinion. Analogically, one might say the same of the Church, only that here there is the additional binding factor of love as incarnated in the person of Christ. But in the end there remains the mys-

[1] "Conciliar Rome," *America*, 112 (March 27, 1965), pp. 420–422.

tery, a mystery discussed in the first chapter of the decree on the Church.

The upgrading of the laity through restoration of the concept of the people of God forced a search, both inside and outside the Council, for new ways to express hierarchical relations and to redefine the functions of the various levels of Church membership. The most obvious, and in many ways the most basic, of these was the reform of the liturgy. The liturgy comprises not only the Mass but the psalms and readings from the Scriptures and Church Fathers, to be sung or recited daily by every priest, and the ceremonies used in administering the sacraments. The Council regarded the subject of such importance as to devote a separate document to spelling out in more detail the principles enunciated in that on the Church.

For the Catholic in the pew, the part of the document that had most immediate pertinence was that dealing with the Mass. Two distinct elements were involved, the form of the Mass and the language in which it should be recited.

As far as the language was concerned, this was not, strictly speaking, an issue for an ecumenical council at all, since the problem existed only in regard to the Latin rite, that part of the Church which comes under the patriarch of the West. The bishop of Rome is not only pope of the universal Church but also one of the five patriarchs set up by early councils, the others being Constantinople, Jerusalem, Antioch, and Alexandria. The languages to be used in the liturgy of each patriarchate are determined by the respective patriarch and his synod. The patriarchates other than Rome normally use a language understood by the people, while allowing for use of ancient languages (Greek, Syrian, etc.) on special occasions.

The bishops, however, decided that the issue of language in the Latin rite was sufficiently important to merit the time of a general council. While retaining Latin as the official language of the rite, it opened the way to the celebration of the Mass and the conferring of the sacraments in other languages. The Council decreed that the national and regional bishops' conferences should decide whether and to what extent the living language was to be used. The point was left deliberately vague in deference to some Fathers who were opposed to any change. The bishops were given full freedom to translate those parts of the

Mass "that concern the people." For the other parts, the bishops must obtain the approval of the Holy See. While some commentators point out that every part of the Mass concerns the people, the clause was officially interpreted in a restrictive sense, limiting the discretion of the bishops to the parts recited or chanted by the people, or those directly addressed to them.

By this action, the Council at least opened the way to ending an anomalous situation that has affected the life of the Roman Church for centuries, one which had become so consecrated by custom that many were opposed to any alteration. The Council pointed out the reasons why change was necessary. All the faithful, it said, are bound to participate with the priest in offering the sacrifice of the Mass, and it is obvious that they cannot do this unless they understand what he is saying and doing. Before the Council, a growing volume of opinion had recognized the logic of this argument, and various methods had been used to increase the involvement of the people in the Mass. The use of individual Missals in the living language had steadily grown. In many parishes there were experiments with commentators or with a reading of the Mass in the vernacular, while the priest used Latin at the altar. But it was the general view of the bishops, as expressed in the debates, that these techniques were not enough. They formed a barrier between priest and people and stressed the artificiality of the solution.

Additional arguments came from missionary bishops of Asia, Africa, and Latin America. Archbishop Eugene D'Souza of India said that the Church must be able "to incarnate itself where it exists," explaining that the local language was a first and essential step toward a much broader adaptation of the rites. A score of others supported him. One of the most telling speeches was that of Maximos IV Saïgh. He pointed out that the very reasons which had brought the Latin rite into existence in Rome in the third century were the same that now required an adaptation both of language and of practices. The people of Rome had no longer understood Greek, so the public prayers of the Church, including the Mass, had been translated into the living language.

When the usages of Rome spread into Germany, France, Spain, and other countries, however, this principle was overlooked. Instead of adaptation, there was a mechanical transfer of the Latin, not a vital transfer of the meaning of the Mass. The priest isolated himself and even turned his back on the people, who developed their private devotions in their own languages, devotions not to be condemned in themselves but often totally unrelated to the Mass. Lay people were encouraged by the clergy to think of their presence at the Mass as an opportunity to develop an isolated, personal spirituality rather than as an expression of community worship.

The sixteenth-century Reformers had turned a spotlight on these issues. They were not against Latin as Latin. What they wanted was a language the people understood so that they could participate. Historically speaking, the failure of Catholics to acknowledge the reasonableness of that request and act accordingly was a major element in the spread of the Reformed Churches.

It was not until Vatican II that Catholics finally faced up to the issue. They did so hesitantly and somewhat ambiguously. Nevertheless, the steps taken there carry the matter to the point of no return. In January 1964, Pope Paul set up a permanent committee in Rome, charged with the duty of completing liturgical reform according to the principles established in the Council decree. This will mean not only an extension of the use of the living language, perhaps to the entire text of the Mass, but a reformation and reformulation of the content of the Mass and other public prayers of the Latin rite. The result will be a liturgy closer to that of the early Church and at the same time more meaningful to twentieth-century man.

The mixture of Latin and the vernacular in the Mass as a first step in liturgical reform was displeasing both to many who favored the living language in the liturgy and to some who would have preferred no change at all. There were, nevertheless, good reasons for the Council's curious mode of action. The limited nature of the immediate change was calculated to soften the blow to the curialists, opposed to any kind of change but especially to a change in their pride and weapon, the Latin language. It was also calculated to soften the emotional impact on the considerable number of Catholics who had regarded Latin as a distinguishing mark of Catholicism and who felt that the use of the living language in church services tended to Protestantize their religion.

Such is the logic of the situation as it existed at the end of the Council. The living language had been introduced to an extent sufficient to establish the principle laid down by the Council and to stress the social and community aspect of public worship. Meanwhile, the committee set up by Pope Paul was giving top priority to a total study of the Latin-rite Mass, with the object of eliminating the unharmonious elements and substituting more appropriate ones. That work was expected to occupy it until about 1970 or perhaps even longer.

Whether it would include a revision of the Canon, the central part of the Mass during which the bread and wine are consecrated as a commemoration and renewal of the Last Supper, is not known. The conservative resistance to such a revision remained great. Pope John XXIII, however, established the principle in favor of revision by inserting the name of St. Joseph in the Canon, the first change in its content in many centuries. Revision of the Canon would seem desirable before its use in the vernacular is introduced; but the use of the vernacular is considered the most necessary change of all, because the Canon is the part of the Mass in which all present are called upon to join with the priest in offering the sacrifice.

Other points on which the Council made hesitant advances concern Holy Communion under the form of both bread and wine and the celebration of Mass together by several priests. Christ at the Last Supper told His disciples to take and eat the bread that was His body *and* the wine that was His blood, and to continue in future to do the same in commemoration of Him. Such was the practice of the early Church and such remains unchanged the practice of the Eastern Churches, both the Orthodox and those in communion with Rome. Largely for practical reasons, the Latin rite restricted the chalice to the officiating priest, giving only the consecrated bread to the people. The sixteenth-century Reformers protested this change, and it became yet another point of conflict.

Vatican II recognized the principle for which the Reformers fought. It provided for reception of both host and chalice in certain great moments of the Catholic's life—by the husband and wife, for example, at the Mass at which they are married. In this way, yet another artificial barrier between cleric and layman was overturned.

The issue of concelebration, or joint celebration of the Mass by several priests, is somewhat technical, yet it affects one's understanding of the nature of the Church. The Mass, as a renewal of the Last Supper, is essentially a social act. Christ called His disciples around Him for a last meal in common before His death. He told them to remember Him later by repeating the same ceremony. Subsequently, if there was but one disciple present with a group of the faithful, he presided over the ceremony and repeated the rituals that Catholics believe transform the bread into the body of Christ and the wine into His blood. But if there were several disciples present, each did not set up a separate banquet table. They all sat down at one table, and all participated in the joint commemoration of the Last Supper.

The practice had all but died out in the Roman rite. One reason was a stress on the personal devotion of the individual priest rather than on the community nature of the service. Another was a mathematical or statistical evaluation, rather than a spiritual one, of the effect of the sacrifice of the Mass. It seemed to some, and the argument was put forward in all seriousness by one of the Fathers on the Council floor, that more honor was given to God and more merit gained for the faithful by several separate than by one joint commemoration.

A further reason undoubtedly was the stipend. The Mass stipend is an offering made to a priest, in return for which he asks God to allocate the spiritual benefits of this Mass in a special way, though not exclusively, for the intentions of the donor of the stipend. The stipend was originally conceived as being the amount of money needed to provide the priest's meals for the day. It is today fixed at different levels from place to place, usually much less than needed for its original purpose. Like many other things in life, it has suffered from the inflationary process. It is, nevertheless, a significant part of the income of many priests, and its outright abolition would cause hardship, especially to missionaries in poverty-stricken lands who receive stipends from Catholics in richer countries. Some fear that the flow of stipends might slow down because many people might mistakenly regard the spiritual benefit from participation in a concelebrated Mass as less than that to be gained from an individual Mass.

The Council moved cautiously but significantly. It established concelebration as the normal and usual way to celebrate Mass on Holy Thursday, the anniversary of the Last Supper. It authorized it in various other situations, as, for example, for priests who live together in a religious community.

A small but voluble minority of Catholics in the United States, France, and elsewhere expressed its opposition to the liturgical reform. Many of the opponents stressed the "Protestantization" of the Church, as though it were somehow disgraceful to proclaim at this late date with Christian humility that in this respect the demands of the Reformers were just. Others found change irksome. They had developed habits and they wanted to die with them. Others again, and this was the biggest problem, had not had the reasons explained to them. They had always been taught that the Church was unchangeable, and suddenly everything was changing. The solid earth of their convictions was turning into quicksand.

In fairness to the Council, however, it must be remembered that it did not pull the new liturgy like a rabbit out of its magician's hat. Much preparation had been made, even if many clerics and laymen had not been looking and listening. As far back as 1903, Pope Pius X called for the active participation of the faithful in the public prayer of the Church. He developed the same concept in his untiring efforts to encourage the practice of frequent reception of the Eucharist by all Catholics. A decisive date for the movement in the United States was 1925, when St. John's Abbey, Collegeville, Minnesota, published the first number of *Orate Fratres*, now titled *Worship*. From this center the movement spread erratically all over the country. In some dioceses, a concern for the liturgy was almost a suspect enthusiasm as late as 1960.

The stress in the early days was on participation in the Gregorian chant, but the Germans in the 1930s began to investigate deeper into the meaning of liturgical piety, stressing the idea of Christians forming a unity in the Mystical Body of Christ. Individual priests were the pioneers, but by 1940 the bishops of Germany had not only become interested but definitely involved.

In those same years, the French were becoming concerned about the decay of religion in their country. A best seller and indeed shocker, published in 1943, entitled *France, pays de Mission?*[2] saw liturgical reform as a necessary step to a religious revival. Finally, Rome was persuaded to make some small concessions. From 1947, evening Masses were authorized in special circumstances. Two years later, as the gate clanged shut in China, the Holy Office authorized the use of Mandarin Chinese for the whole Mass except the Canon. But it was too late (some would say three centuries too late), for the world's history might have been very different if Rome had not in the seventeenth century condemned the so-called Chinese rites, the adaptation by the Jesuits of Catholic practice to Chinese culture.

The disaster in China no doubt helped the advance of liturgical reform elsewhere. About 1950 came authorization to use the living language in some rituals, as in the conferring of certain sacraments and in the reform of the ceremonies of Holy Saturday. Still later came the shortening of the period of fasting before receiving the Eucharist and an extension of the authorization for evening Mass. The Council, consequently, did no more than speed up a process that had already taken clear shape and direction.

A much more complicated problem remains, one that will probably take several generations to resolve fully. The Latin rite has spread today far beyond the area whose basic culture derives from Greece and Rome. To make it meaningful for us in the West, formed in Western thought patterns, it needs only translation and updating. But for the Christians of Asia and Africa and for the vast numbers of Latin Americans who have never come effectively within the orbit of Western culture, much more is needed. In this non-Aristotelian world, one must begin afresh, and as Archbishop Jean Baptiste Zoa of Yaoundé says, the starting point must not be Western practice but the Scriptures. Indeed, the thought patterns of many of these peoples are much nearer those of the Scripture writers than are ours, as one may verify by comparing the book of Job with one of the classics of Zen Buddhism.

2 Henri Godin and René Michel. Translated into English and adapted by Maisie Ward as *France, Pagan?* (New York, Sheed & Ward, 1949.)

The decree, in fact, lays the groundwork for such basic re-formulation. As Archbishop Zoa said, it calls for an approach based on the genius of each people. The development must pass through three stages: the reception of the tradition, its assimilation, and its vital re-expression. Thus, he suggested, for the rite of Baptism Africans should return to immersion as practiced in the early Church, and indeed as practiced by John the Baptist. For the secondary rites, African equivalents must be sought, a work calling for the help of specialists in anthropology and ethnology, and taking care to avoid the fossilization of ceremonies that the people are abandoning as they enter the modern world in their own way.

Bishop Lawrence Satoshi Nagae, of Urawa, Japan, agreed with these principles while stressing how delicate the process of application is. The Japanese, he said, are not against everything Western. On the contrary, they have shown an amazing facility for incorporating much of Western civilization without losing their own culture. But they resist some elements. Unlike the Latin American, the Japanese dislikes being touched by another. Accordingly, the so-called kiss of peace, which is really an embrace rather than a kiss in the usual sense of the word, is distasteful to them and has already been eliminated from the Mass in Japan. Similarly, the Japanese bow instead of genuflecting, because it is natural for them to bow but humiliating to genuflect.

Marriage ceremonies offer an excellent example of the need of adaptation. Here a start has already been made. Thus, the Tamils of Ceylon place the *thali* around the neck instead of putting a ring on the finger. But all of this adaptation can be completed only when the Churches of the so-called mission countries are no longer dominated by Western missionaries or by local clerics trained by those missionaries to despise the traditions of their own peoples. Such a mistaken formation has been given in many places. With the best of intentions, the missionaries removed the young boys from their families before the time of initiation into the tribe. They brought them up in schools and seminaries with minimum contact with their own people. Seeing it with their mentors' eyes, they tended to judge their own culture as inferior and barbaric. Such men, who are admirable and dedicated priests and bishops today according to their lights, are no more capable of making other than provisional and superficial adaptations than are the outsiders. We must wait for a new generation of priests formed within their own culture and proud of it.

The restored dignity of the laity as full members of the people of God encouraged and, indeed, forced the rethinking of many concepts long accepted as definitely established. Even before the Council ended, new formulations of their obligations were being sought by theologians in a less legalistic, pontifical spirit. The Fathers themselves repeatedly insisted that the Church did not have, here and now, the answer to every question, not even to every question for which many of its members might be compelled to give an answer, and that in such circumstances it was for the individual to make the best judgment he himself could form in his own situation. The result was thus a new stress on the existentialist elements in human judgments, as opposed to a tendency in recent centuries to give glib answers to artificially simplified questions.

As of yet, there has been but timid and token implementation of the principle of lay participation in the daily life of the Church, far short of Orthodox and Protestant practice, more tactical than substantive. A few bishops in the United States have set up advisory committees of the laity to help guide them in running their dioceses. But often the stress is on advice in handling the business affairs of the diocese, thus reviving in practice a principle rejected by the Council, namely, that the special competence of the cleric is the spiritual, and of the layman, the temporal. The Council, on the contrary, insisted that all the affairs of the Church are the joint concern of all the people of God.

Another curious development in the United States is a growth of antilaicism among the clergy. Encouraged by the principles enunciated by the Council, educated Catholic laymen have begun to speak their minds and make their decisions with a previously unknown freedom. The change finds supporters among some of the younger clergy, but it shocks those bishops, priests, and nuns who were accustomed to treating all under their jurisdiction as children. The specific issue concerns the meaning of obedience. In the past, Catholic seminaries and schools taught and imposed what they called blind obedience.

If the one in authority made a decision, then all under his authority were supposed to obey unquestioningly, even if the decision was arbitrary. Many are now saying that obedience requires the use of one's reason, that it must be a personal commitment preceded by reflection and judgment. Accordingly, the archbishop of Los Angeles was widely challenged when he sought to restrict Catholic participation in the fight for racial justice. Professors in St. John's University in New York formed a union and demanded a larger share in administration policy. Students in a Midwest seminary staged a "pray-in" to protest that the theology being taught them in their classes was unduly conservative.

The new approach to obedience is not original. All that is sought is that the more sophisticated concept of obedience practiced in today's office, shop, and factory—a technique for achieving co-operation and performance more in accord with man's dignity—be applied also in the Church, thereby avoiding the schizophrenic division of the man and the believer. This, its advocates insist, is not a lower but a higher form of obedience. It demands the constant exercise of man's highest faculties in the performance of his duties.

Clerics formed in the old concepts find it hard to grasp what is happening. Confused and uncertain, fearful of losing their hold on the situation, some simplify everything to a crisis of obedience. The reaction can be seen in the editorials of many Catholic newspapers and magazines, most of which are owned by the bishops or the various religious orders. The issue exists not only for the laity but also for the religious orders of men and women. Many of their members are as determined as are the laity to update and (as they see it) purify the concept of obedience in their convents and monasteries.

During the early part of the Council, Catholic publications were virtually unanimous in welcoming the restoration of the notion of the people of God as actively participating in the whole life of the Church. Now, as they see the efforts of the people of God to assert their admitted rights, they are frightened. Sometimes, one can sympathize with them. The laity has been passive for so long that its functions have been atrophied. When it tries to walk, it limps. When it tries to speak, its control of its vocal chords can be uncertain, producing off-key screams. But to call this a crisis of obedience is wide of the mark. At most, there is a crisis of confidence. Of course, bad handling by those in authority could make it something worse.

Chapter 5

Humility
Leads to Unity

All Christians everywhere have always agreed that Christ wanted His followers to be one, as He and the Father are one. In spite of this, few facts have been more evident for centuries than the progressive fragmentation of Christendom into warring sects, divided not only by conflicting beliefs but by lack of love for each other.

This is not to say that Christians were entirely unconcerned. Each group found a formula to rationalize its position. For the Roman Catholic, the matter was simple. He had the fullness of truth, and the others had strayed away. It was for them to recognize their error and return to the fold, where they would be forgiven and readmitted. The Orthodox took a similar line. Roman Catholicism had erred by adding to, and at times changing, the faith formulated by the early Councils. Only the entire Church was entitled to add to what these Councils had decided. Let the Roman Catholics abrogate their unilateral actions, then join with Orthodoxy in making whatever new decisions might be necessary.

The Protestant position was usually more subtle. It stressed the bond of faith and charity in the Church while playing down the visible links—the authority and the structures—in favor of the right of each person to interpret the Scriptures for himself. It consequently could envisage a multiplicity of sects without a substantive division of the unity demanded by Christ. It could even see the possibility of encompassing Orthodoxy within its framework. But it generally had to face the dilemma of a Roman Catholicism unassimilable to its formula by reason of its own intransigent insistence on a contradictory one.

Protestants, nevertheless, gradually came to see that theological and practical reasons demanded a reversal of the fragmentation, so they urged organic relationships among existing Christian bodies. The need was clearest in mission lands, where the conflicting claims of different Christian bodies hindered the spread of Christianity and scandalized non-Christians. A world missions conference at Edinburgh, Scotland, in 1910, witnessed the first attempts of Protestants to rationalize mission efforts by agreement on division of territories. This work progressed to such an extent as to justify the setting up of an International Missions Council as a permanent body in 1921.

Co-operation in mission lands also gradually affected attitudes in the traditional Christian countries, and the idea of a fellowship of Churches took concrete form in 1937, when two ecumenical conferences elected a joint committee to formulate plans for a world council. The Second World War delayed the completion of the committee's work, and it was not until 1948 that the first assembly of the World Council of Churches was held, with participation of Protestant, Anglican, and Orthodox members. The success of this body has been phenomenal. Various Protestant groups have over the years agreed on a common formulation of faith, and the movement toward greater organizational unity continues at an accelerated pace.

Although the World Council's constitutions were carefully worded to protect the conscience and beliefs of each member Church, Rome continued to hold haughtily aloof. Individual Catholic theologians, like French Dominican Yves Congar, who tried to prepare Catholics to understand the positive content of this movement, were harassed by Rome's censors. Only with Pope John's help were Catholics able to analyze objectively and openly the facts of the division of Christians, to recognize a common blame both for the divisions and for their continuance, and to propose new approaches to a solution.

That deep theological issues divide Christians, all parties agree. But the issues must be kept in perspective. Christopher

Dawson's recent book on Church unity concludes that the main sources of Christian division and the chief obstacles to Christian unity are "cultural rather than theological." Each party to the conflict, he says, has its own version of history, its social inheritance, its own religious beliefs and standards of orthodoxy.[1]

Catholics and Protestants alike have had their religious history conditioned for 400 years by the break in the sixteenth century. Their theology has been cast in such supposedly conflicting polarities as faith versus works, word versus sacrament, and freedom versus authority. Their systems of philosophy have taken different roads. Catholics have clung desperately to the rigidities of Scholasticism, admitting at most the cautious updatings of the Neo-Scholastics. Protestants have gone along with the currents of post-Reformation secular thought.

The late Gustave Weigel, S.J., once presented the resultant situation in an amusing comparison. Some wag, he wrote, has defined basic epistemological positions in terms of a baseball umpire calling strikes and balls. The Scholastic umpire calls them as they are. The Kantian subjectivist calls them as he sees them. The Existentialist umpire insists that they are what he calls them. And, concluded Father Weigel, the Protestant is by and large a subjectivist with a strong leaning toward Existentialism. One can see the area for semantic confusion between him and a Catholic trained in Scholastic formalism.[2]

Orthodoxy was not involved in the conflict between the Reformers and Rome. Its unhappy memories are concerned rather with the ruptures in the realm of charity and of political loyalties that grew up gradually from the sixth or seventh century and were not consummated until the fifteenth. Such differences as separated the parties in the religious areas were mostly incidental, excuses rather than issues.

Roman Emperor Constantine the Great, blamed by many at Vatican II for having begun the church-state association that has since been traditional in Roman Catholic theory and practice, also set in motion the forces that led to the division of Christians into Orthodox and Roman Catholics. His transfer of

[1] *The Dividing of Christendom* (New York, Sheed & Ward, 1965).

[2] Robert McAfee Brown and Gustave Weigel, S.J., *An American Dialogue* (New York, Doubleday & Co., 1960), p. 157.

the seat of empire from Rome to Byzantium, renamed Constantinople, set up a second center of power in the Church. The bishop of Constantinople was soon to be recognized as a patriarch with precedence over the other patriarchs except the pope, patriarch of the West.

The gap between Rome and Constantinople grew wider in the Dark Ages. Unable to count on help from Constantinople in its struggle with the new peoples threatening its northern and western borders, Rome turned to alliances with these long-time enemies. The crowning of the Frankish leader Charlemagne as Roman emperor by the pope was viewed as treason by Constantinople. It no longer saw the pope as the father and symbol of Christian unity, a conviction confirmed when the Crusaders proved less effective as opponents of the Saracens than as the spearhead of Western expansionism and colonization. The pope, their leader and inspirer, remained for the Orthodox only as a hated political symbol after the Crusaders in 1204 sacked Constantinople and destroyed whatever potential the Eastern Empire still had to withstand the Moslem Saracens.

From that time onward, the unity discussions were motivated on both sides more by politics than by religion. Rome wanted to restore herself as the seat of Empire and effect the cultural absorption of the Eastern Christians by imposing on them her centralized ecclesiastical control. The Orthodox considered the price too high, but accepted it at the Councils of Lyons and Florence in return for protection against burgeoning Islam. When Rome failed to perform her part of the bargain, allowing Constantinople to fall to the Turks in 1453, the rest of the agreement was doomed.

Nor did the cultural conflict end at this point in historical time. As the Orthodox see it, that conflict has continued down through the centuries, a powerful Rome taking advantage of the weakness of the Orthodox communities living in most part in the underdeveloped and hostile environment of Islamic nations. It must be remembered that Islam dominated not only the Orthodox and other Eastern Christians of Asia Minor and Egypt, but, for centuries, those of the Balkans as well. Even when the Moslems were driven out of all of Europe except Constantinople (Istanbul) itself in the nineteenth and twentieth centuries, they left behind them poor and divided countries in which Rome (as the Orthodox see it) continued to play her old game. Specifically, she promoted the formation of separate communities (the so-called Uniats), performing the same religious rites as the Orthodox but acknowledging dependence on Rome in a way in which it was never professed or practiced by Eastern Christians even before the split. These communities, subsidized by Rome, urge their fellow Orthodox to reject their errors and return to the unity of the true faith.

This emotional grievance of the Orthodox must be understood by the West before significant dialogue can begin, to say nothing of unity. It is most acute in Greece, still smarting from Mussolini's invasion during World War II, an aggression interpreted by the Orthodox as a continuation of the thousand-year-old policy of absorption. But it also comes up in every conversation in Istanbul, Jerusalem, and Cairo. "Imagine what a scandal it would be to you, if we started similar divisive activities in your countries," a member of the Holy Synod of Patriarch Athenagoras said to this writer in Istanbul. "We could easily do it, you know. We could put on Roman collars, say Mass in the Latin rite, begin to preach in France or Italy, or wherever we might decide. We could honestly tell the people that we are true priests, as we are, that we accept the primacy of the pope, as we do. We could win converts to our position. But would we advance Christianity? We believe not, and we believe that neither does Rome by its similar techniques in our countries."

It is in this context that one must evaluate such intransigent statements as those of Archbishop Chrysostomos of Athens, who even in 1965 could proclaim: "While I'm alive, there will be no approach to Rome." But it would also be wrong to assume that he speaks for Orthodoxy. On the contrary, there has been an extraordinarily rapid evolution of thought, even in Greece. The great spokesman in Athens for a new unprejudiced approach to Rome is the famous theologian and canonist, Professor Amilkas Alivizatos. He is a layman, like many leading Orthodox theologians. Though now very old, he is still a moral and intellectual force in the country. Backing him are such people as the Zoë Society, a group of priests and laymen engaged in a program to modernize Orthodox monasticism. Active among young people, they have derived much inspiration from the Pax Romana organizations for university students and other intellectuals and from movements like the young Christian Workers, started in Belgium by Cardinal Cardijn and now widespread in Western Europe, the two Americas, and Africa.

The man who more than any other has persuaded the Orthodox that God calls them to an immediate return in charity and ultimate return in formal union to the rest of Christianity is his Holiness Athenagoras I, Patriarch of Constantinople. He is one who performed for Orthodoxy miracles like those Pope John performed for Roman Catholicism. Born in northern Greece in 1886, in an area that was then Turkish, he made early contact with the West when he served as a chaplain in Yugoslavia in World War I. Considerably later, he spent 17 years (1931–48) in the United States as archbishop of the Americas. During that time he brought together a divided and decaying Orthodox Church, instilling in it the vigor and sense of unity it has since retained. He was always ecumenical in outlook and actions, with Protestants and Catholics alike. He happily recalls that long before his historic embrace with Pope Paul in the Holy Land, Cardinal Cushing of Boston and he caused a sensation in the United States when they embraced publicly in the presence of photographers.

Athenagoras was reluctant to return to Istanbul. The patriarchate had, since World War I and the establishment of modern Turkey, fallen to a low ebb. A dwindling handful of Christians in the hostile Moslem environment formed its only direct support. There was internal discord, and a majority in the governing body, the Holy Synod, had no liking for Athenagoras' ecumenical novelties. On the other hand, he saw (as he still sees) the Western world and particularly the two Americas as currently the most promising area for an expansion of Orthodoxy. The 14 independent but co-operating Orthodox Churches in the United States had several million adherents living in a pluralist situation quite novel to them. Thanks to the initiatives of Athenagoras, their leaders were seeking adaptation. The missionary drive, widespread in Russian Orthodoxy in the seventeenth to the nineteenth centuries, was reviving. Athenagoras wondered if he should abandon his work in America for something so tenuous as the historic patriarchate.

One of his many prominent friends helped him decide. "You can do more for Christian reunion there," the then President of the United States, Harry Truman, urged him. He went back to Istanbul in 1949, in an airplane provided by the U.S. government, and gradually persuaded the Holy Synod to work internally for a more organic unity of the Orthodox and externally for Church union. Like Pope John, he sees unity as a fruit of love expressing itself with Christian humility. His own life is a perfect example of his beliefs. No comic-opera soldiers or plainclothes detectives guard the Phanar, his residence in Istanbul. No footmen serve his simple food and watered wine when he sits to a simple meal with a guest.

Athenagoras would like to move much faster ecumenically than he has done, but he can move only at the speed of Orthodox agreement. To think of him as an Eastern pope would be to misunderstand a basic difference between Roman Catholicism and Orthodoxy. His primacy is primarily one of honor. For his own Church, he is chairman of the board, the board being the twelve-man Holy Synod. Each Orthodox Church—Russian, Greek, Rumanian, and so on—has its own board. In recent centuries, these Churches have had little administrative coordination, stressing only a unity of doctrine and worship. Athenagoras has made significant progress by developing a permanent organ of consultation, important for negotiations with Rome, but he must move within his tradition.

For several reasons, Athenagoras is not anxious for theological discussions with Rome right now. For one thing, his advisers do not think that Orthodoxy could field a team able to meet a Roman team on a level of equality. Orthodoxy has lived too long in the underdeveloped world. It lacks the great universities, libraries, research facilities, and graduate schools of the Christian West. As a member of the Holy Synod said, "What we need now is your technical assistance. You must place us on a level of equality before we can negotiate as equals."

For another thing, Athenagoras does not see theology as the place to start. "It is my job to protect the purity of the deposit of faith," he has said. "But I am not a theologian, nor for this do I need to be. Let us find ourselves as brothers, as Pope Paul and I did in the Holy Land, and later the theologians can work out their own problems."

He would begin with such practical discussions as spiritual and liturgical renewal, social questions, and peace. He sees the East and the West as the two halves of the Church, each obliged to discover in the other the potential it lacks from the very fact of being split down the middle.

Some of the Orthodox, led by intransigents in Greece, do not believe that any progress can be made even at the practical level unless some issues of doctrine and practice are first clarified. The papal primacy looms large among the stumbling blocks. The Orthodox admit a primacy of honor, but reject a universal papal jurisdiction over the Church. The Eastern mind reacts similarly against Roman legalism. Changes introduced by the West without the consent of the Orthodox also cause troubles, for example, the addition of the *filioque* to the Athanasian Creed and the definition of the Immaculate Conception and Assumption of the Blessed Virgin Mary. Many on the Western side are convinced, nevertheless, and some Orthodox theologians seem to agree, that these are primarily issues of procedure. The Orthodox are not so much challenging the beliefs as the mode of formulation and the unilateral character of the West's action.

Vatican II has provided a significantly better climate for continued approaches to each other by Rome and Orthodoxy. A first step was the way Pope John invited observers to the Council. Some had hoped for an invitation to the Orthodox as full members, as at Basle and Constance, but leaders on both sides saw that the emotional and juridical bases for such confrontation did not exist. Even the invitation to send observers, although cordially received by Athenagoras, had slight practical results at the start. But the number of Orthodox official observers and personal representatives grew steadily with each session. Their presence contributed to an awareness of the Orthodox positions among the Fathers and to serious efforts—not always successful—to take them into account.

Positive achievements of the Council include the statement on collegiality. Orthodoxy has always stressed the importance of local synods, paralleling today's stress by the West on national and regional conferences of bishops as an implementation of the concept of collegiality. The over-all emphasis on charity as the bond of union of the Church, expressed in the decree on the Church and in other documents, is pleasing to the Orthodox as an antidote to Western legalism and insistence on hierarchical authority.

The decree on ecumenism carries things considerably farther. It proclaims the Catholic Church's belief that the Christian Churches, especially those of Orthodoxy, are still essentially united in spite of their differences. "Men who believe in Christ and have been truly baptized are in real communion with the Catholic Church, even though this union is imperfect." As for the Orthodox, the decree warns the West against any idea of "Westernizing" them as a part of the process of reunion. On the contrary, it insists that we must always remember "the character of the relations which obtained between them and the Roman See before separation." The Orthodox, the decree further affirms explicitly, "possess true sacraments and above all, by apostolic succession, the priesthood and the Eucharist, whereby they are linked with us in closest intimacy. Therefore some worship in common [*communicatio in sacris*], given suitable circumstances and the approval of Church authority, is not merely possible but to be encouraged."

The decree incorporates the most explicit protection of the jurisdictional autonomy of the Eastern Churches in anticipation of later corporate reunion. "From the earliest times the Eastern Churches followed their own forms of ecclesiastical law and custom, which were sanctioned by the approval of the Fathers of the Church, of synods, and even of ecumenical councils. Far from being an obstacle to the Church's unity, such diversity of customs and observances only adds to its comeliness, and is of great help in carrying out its mission, as has already been stated. To remove, then, all shadow of doubt, this holy synod solemnly declares that the Churches of the East, while remembering the necessary unity of the whole Church, have the power and duty to govern themselves according to the disciplines proper to them, since these are better suited to the character of their faithful, and more for the good of their souls. The perfect observance of this principle which, for all its periodical neglect, is sanctioned by long-standing tradition, is one of the essential prerequisites for any restoration of unity."

Cardinal Lercaro, Archbishop of Bologna, Italy, has summed up the significance of these and other passages in the decree.

They mean, he says, that from the Catholic viewpoint, the marks of the true Church are substantially present in our brothers of the Orthodox East, even though still incompletely in our eyes. The Orthodox have preserved intact the apostolic faith and succession, and the reality of the sacraments. The resulting communion between Catholics and Orthodox, which is not only permitted but recommended in certain cases, cannot —concludes the cardinal—but be an authentic participation in the communion of the true Church of Christ.[3]

The apparent meaning of all this is that the Catholic Church has gone "solemnly" on record as being prepared to enter into an immediate union of worship with the Orthodox, without demanding from them in return any formal change in their present proclaimed beliefs and practices. The implementation of such a proposal, however, obviously needs a similar willingness on the other side. That this cannot be ruled out is clear from a recent statement of Professor P. Afanasyev of the Orthodox Theological Institute of Paris. It is possible, he said, to restore Eucharistic communion before full dogmatic unity. The break between East and West was, in his view, more a failure in charity than a breach in doctrine, and in the increased union nurtured by the sacrament of charity, the Roman See would gradually regain its old position of primacy in love. "The dogmatic differences, now seemingly insuperable, would be lifted to the light of this charity. . . . Once charity was placed above knowledge, knowledge too would become more perfect."[4]

The same viewpoint was expressed by two distinguished United States churchmen in an interview published in *The Denver Catholic Register* after the promulgation of the Council's decree. Cardinal Cushing of Boston and Greek Orthodox Archbishop Demetrios Iakovos agreed that intercommunion could be anticipated in a few years, even before formal unity. It seems legitimate to conclude that the actual date of reunion of East and West may never be recorded in any document or even precisely fixed, that it will be a gradual growing together,

[3] The text of Cardinal Lercaro's talk is reproduced in *Herder Correspondence,* Vol. 2, No. 5 (May 1965).

[4] Quoted by Eugene C. Bianchi, S.J., in *America,* 111 (November 28, 1964), pp. 688–691.

just as the schism was a gradual growing apart. In any case, the decision by the Council to permit worship in common in approved situations is a decisive step toward that goal. For the East, the whole Church is realized locally in the action of the Eucharistic assembly, so that the sacramental mystery has at once canonical, liturgical, theological, and institutional dimensions.

Not everything the Council did, however, was equally calculated to please the Orthodox. There was still too much talk of powers, rights, and privileges in many Council documents and speeches. In addition, the determination of Rome to run the affairs of the Eastern Churches, even while it proclaims that they are autonomous, continued in full force.

The prime example of this contradictory attitude was the decree on the Eastern Churches. This was legislation only for the less than 5 per cent of Eastern Christians who acknowledge the primacy of the pope and maintain formal communion with Rome. Its purpose was to modify some of the recent Roman legislation contrary to the traditions of these Churches and designed to bring them closer to Latin practices. It restored, for example, the Eastern custom by virtue of which priests administer the sacrament of Confirmation. It made it possible to contract valid marriage without the canonical form fixed in the West, that is to say, without the presence of the pastor of the Catholic party or his delegate. It authorized Eastern Catholic priests to give the sacraments to Orthodox who ask for them and also authorized Catholics to ask Orthodox priests for the sacraments in case of "necessity or real spiritual benefit." It was only recently that Rome had forbidden these practices, but many Eastern Catholic clerics and lay people were in fact ignoring the prohibition.

While the Eastern Christians welcomed these concessions by Rome, they could only be disturbed by a deeper issue. By what right was the West, which dominated the Council, legislating for the East? The decree on ecumenism had explicitly stated that the Churches of the East had "the power and duty" to govern themselves. In addition, they claimed, the decree presented the Eastern Churches as special cases, as though the Western Church was really the entire Church and the others a sort of historical oddity or appendage. Moreover, it was improper to impose a uniform legislation on a series of Eastern Churches, each with its distinct history, traditions, and current problems.

On top of all of this, there was the burning question of the patriarchs. The office of patriarch goes back to the earliest times and was known in the whole Church. The basic concept of the patriarchs as the top rulers of the Church is already found in one of the canons of the Council of Nicea (325). Emperor Justinian set up their civil status in the Roman Empire and gave the name of patriarch to the bishops of five dioceses: Rome, Constantinople, Alexandria, Antioch, and Jerusalem. Later, with the expansion of Christianity in Russia and the rising importance of Russia as a secular power, Moscow was added.

For most Eastern Christians, the patriarchate is still the institution decreed by the early Councils. They were not satisfied that the decree on the Eastern Churches recognized it as the traditional form of Church government in the East, giving the patriarch jurisdiction over all bishops of his territory or rite and the right to name Church dignitaries in his territory. They wanted, as Patriarch Maximos IV Saïgh pleaded, to have the patriarchate recognized for the universal Church, with the pope included as patriarch of the West and all the patriarchs proclaimed as the summits of the universal episcopate, in conformity with Church practice before the division.

The real issue here, although not spelled out in so many words, is the relation of patriarchs and cardinals. The cardinalate has been the dominant structure of authority in Roman Catholicism since the eleventh century, but historically it is a much less important Church institution than the patriarchate. As Thomas E. Bird has noted in *Commonweal*, its rests on a tenuous legal basis, and it is a blatant and historically offensive expression of Roman triumphalism.[5] Although Pope Eugene IV, in a moment of rhetoric, proclaimed the office as "instituted by St. Peter himself," and ordered that prelates so honored should take precedence before all patriarchs, archbishops, and bishops, the cardinalate is not even conferred by the pope as such but by the bishop of Rome for the government of his

[5] "Red Hats and Red Flags," 82 (March 26, 1965), pp. 9–13.

diocese of Rome. At least such was the situation until 1965, when Pope Paul made a change (to be explained below) designed to transform the college of cardinals into an institution for the whole Church.

The issue of precedence came up at Vatican II, as it had come up in previous Councils. The organizers had followed the instruction of canon law, which ranks cardinals first. But Maximos IV Saïgh and other patriarchs continued to protest, and finally a compromise was worked out. The cardinals and the patriarchs were seated on opposite sides of the floor and on platforms of equal height. Pope John had earlier softened the ruling of Eugene IV by ordering that all cardinals should be made bishops, thus eliminating the shock of a priest preceding a bishop.

Strong forces, nevertheless, seek to retain the status of cardinals as the supreme consultative body with the pope. Another move in this direction was the naming in early 1965 of most of the Eastern patriarchs in union with Rome as cardinals, thus giving them a small voice in an organization expanded to a membership of over a hundred.

The plan had been envisaged for some time and had been vigorously opposed by the Easterns. Maximos IV Saïgh, an outspoken defender of the East, loved and respected by the Orthodox and one of the leading lights of Vatican II, had several times refused the cardinalate. Archbishop Elias Zoghby, vicar of Maximos for Egypt, said that the patriarch's synod had discussed the matter and had decreed that Eastern-rite patriarchs could be members of the college of cardinals only by virtue of their patriarchate, and that the patriarchs would have to be at the top of the college of cardinals or any other universal central organism of the Church.

When Maximos did, in fact, accept the cardinalate without fulfillment of these conditions, the Melchites were astonished and ecumenists were shocked, knowing the negative effect this would produce on the Orthodox. Maximos resisted to the end. He reluctantly yielded, he said, because the college of cardinals had been developed into an institution for the whole Church and was no longer a structure of the diocese of Rome, because he could not resist the pope's plea, and because the pope had recognized the precedence of the patriarchs over all the cardinals other than the six so-called suburbicarian.[6] But even at the ceremony of investiture, he did not genuflect or kiss the pope's ring (forms foreign to the Eastern rituals), nor did he put on the ring or biretta when he received them.

The over-all reaction of the Orthodox is that they have witnessed at the Council a change of heart in the Catholic Church but that the Roman mind remains in its imperial, legalistic, occidental mold. And at least some of them recognize with Father René Laurentin that the approval of the offending decree on the Eastern Churches was won by control of the mechanisms of the Council against the sense of the Council itself. They also recognize that the progress, however limited, carries the issues farther than the wildest dreams of five years earlier, that even the doors that have been closed have not been barred.

Reacting positively to this progress, the Orthodox have themselves made significant advances toward internal consensus with a view to formal dialogue with Rome. The Rhodes Conference of November 1964 revealed the extent of internal agreement, while also revealing some of the major obstacles. Thus, political concerns weighed heavily on the participants. The Churches of Eastern Europe are unable to enter binding agreements likely to displease their civil rulers. The Russians continue to suspect anything that might stress the primacy of Constantinople. The Rumanians see the Vatican as a capitalistic state. The spokesmen of Antioch are worried about the negative Arab reaction to the statement on the Jews.

In spite of all this, very positive decisions were taken. As summarized by Metropolitan Nikodim of Leningrad, each Orthodox Church agreed to study the issues of dialogue with Rome from its own position, following which all of them would meet again to reach a common decision to begin theological discussions. Meanwhile, each Church was authorized to start its own "brotherly," that is, nondogmatic, relations with Rome. In the meantime, the burden is laid on Rome not to take advantage of its strength as against the weakness of the many small Orthodox parties. While it might win tactical gains here and there, it would not achieve anything permanent. In the

[6] Designating the highest rank in the college of cardinals, each being a bishop of a diocese adjoining Rome.

end, only a united Orthodoxy can make truly binding agreements.

The close of the Council was marked by a significant ecumenical gesture. On December 7, 1965, a joint declaration was published in Rome and in Istanbul canceling the mutual excommunications formulated in 1054. In that year, Cardinal Humbertus, as papal legate, excommunicated Patriarch Michael Cerularius, and the patriarch replied by excommunicating the pope. The original intention was to censure only the individuals named on both sides, but the ultimate effect was to break ecclesiastical communion between East and West.

In the joint declaration, Pope Paul and Patriarch Athenagoras expressed regret for "the offensive words, the reproaches without foundation, and the reprehensible gestures" on both sides. They regretted and removed "both from memory and from the midst of the Church the sentences of excommunication which followed those events." They hoped that the whole Christian world would see the gesture as an expression of their common desire to grow toward "that full communion of faith, fraternal accord, and sacramental life which existed among them during the first thousand years of the life of the Church."

The Council contributed to a parallel improvement in relations between Rome and the Churches that sprang from the sixteenth-century Reformation. The climate for such improvement had been growing for some time. As Hans Küng has pointed out, both Catholics and Protestants had grown accustomed to schism. First, they had fought wars. Later, they had reconciled themselves to an indefinite cold war. Their books, newspapers, violent words, and loveless deeds presented fellow Christians as though they were men without God, or so estranged them that they usually knew each other only from the outside and from a distorted perspective.

The two World Wars, and particularly the persecution from Fascist and Red dictatorships, had changed this climate in Europe. Christians rediscovered each other in bomb shelters, jails, concentration camps. They found that they revered in common the same God and Father, the same Lord Jesus Christ, the same Baptism, the same word of God in the Scriptures, the same Lord's Prayer.

On the Catholic side, as already noted, the expression of such sentiments was rigidly controlled until the pontificate of John XXIII. But once the lid came off, the depth of the desire to face issues and recognize the broad areas of agreement could no longer be ignored. Small groups of Council Fathers, mostly from traditionally Catholic countries which still count on polemics to retain the allegiance of the ignorant masses, remained opposed. It was, nevertheless, the constant concern of the great majority of the Fathers to recognize the mistakes on the Catholic side, to wipe away the prejudices and incorrect evaluations, to isolate the differences of substance between the parties, and to develop machinery to deal with these in a Christian manner.

Substantive differences between Catholics and the Reformed Churches are more numerous and more serious than those between Catholics and Orthodox. Each of the Reformed Churches —Lutheranism, Calvinism, Anglicanism, and their many derivatives—has its special beliefs and viewpoints. All in general reject the Catholic concept of the pope's primacy and particularly of his infallibility as defined at Vatican I. They regard the Catholic devotion to Mary as grossly exaggerated and as threatening to elevate her finally to the level of the Trinity or substitute her for Christ as the fountain of grace. They reject the view common in Roman Catholicism, at least in recent centuries, of two sources of revelation: Scripture and Tradition. For them, all revealed truth is in the Bible. They resist the legalism and formalism of modern Roman Catholicism, influenced at least in part by a different philosophical approach to formulation of the issues. As already noted, Catholic teaching is almost invariably presented in Scholastic terms and by theologians trained in the precision of Scholastic terminology. The spokesmen of the Reformed Churches for the most part abhor Scholasticism and are trained in the more flexible and self-questioning philosophies current in the Western world today.

But perhaps the strongest and deepest of the Reformation's objections to Rome was and is the Catholic concept of the Church as a human intermediary between God's majesty and man's conscience. Closely related is the question of whether salvation is by faith alone or by faith plus good works. Luther accused Rome of teaching Pelagianism. He insisted it taught that man could by his own efforts attain salvation, and he was able to support his argument by pointing to contemporary Catholic practices related to pious works and indulgences. Those practices, which represented a serious deformation of Catholic teaching, were not condemned until 40 years later by the Council of Trent. And, as a passing discussion at the Second Vatican Council brought to light, the Catholic theology on indulgences remained confused even after Trent and is still far from clear.

By the time the Council of Trent had finally begun to meet the more serious of Luther's criticisms, the theological controversies and religious wars had so inflamed passions that it proved impossible to restore the lost balance. Instead, what emerged was the so-called Church of the Counter Reformation. Against the Reformers' stress on the spiritual bond of unity among believers, Rome stressed the hierarchical elements and produced the top-heavy clericalized Church of the nineteenth and twentieth centuries. The Reformers insisted on the universal priesthood of all believers, but some of them carried it to an extreme unacceptable to Catholics by denying a special priesthood of the ordained minister. Catholics reacted by limiting the laity to passive participation in the Mass and other official prayers.

The first and perhaps the biggest thing Vatican II did in this area was to open up all Catholic positions to honest and objective analysis. This was the great surprise and delight of the non-Roman observers, official and unofficial. By the final session of the Council, the number of delegates, substitutes, and guests from the Reformed Churches had grown to nearly 100. They attended all meetings of the Fathers, received all documents, had the service of simultaneous translators, and were encouraged to discuss their problems with the Council Fathers and theological experts. Although they did not participate in the debates, their views were often more influential than those of the speakers.

Gradually it emerged that behind the apparent inflexibility of the Catholic front, there had always existed a great variety of positions, many of them much more acceptable to Protestant theologians than the "official" Catholic teaching. Thus, the proclamation of the collegiality of the bishops in the decree on the nature of the Church placed Vatican I's definition of papal infallibility in a new light. Instead of an individual elevated to a pinnacle of personal inerrancy, it had become possible to envisage the pope as the spokesman for an infallible Church to which he was organically bound as head of the college of bishops.

The upgrading of the laity as full members of the people of God and the express affirmation of their common priesthood in Baptism, as presented in the decrees on the liturgy and on the lay apostolate, also served to meet the legitimate criticisms of the Reformers.

Further progress was registered in the decree on ecumenism. In an analysis from the Protestant viewpoint, Robert McAfee Brown acclaimed the great headway revealed in this document. It officially endorsed views, he said, that were not even discussed in public when the Council opened. He found it particularly significant that the Fathers during the debates added elements that the Secretariat for Christian Unity had omitted for fear of trying to go too far too fast. In its anxiety not to crystallize a solid opposition, the secretariat had underestimated the favorable temper of the bishops.

Specifically, the decree acknowledged that Catholics, as well as Protestants, shared the responsibility for the scandal of division. It admitted that the Catholic Church on earth was not perfect, that on the contrary, Christ summoned it "to continual reformation." This was a significant act of humility on the part of the Council. Earlier Catholic apologists had stubbornly refused to countenance the claim of Luther that the Church as such needed to be reformed.

Another important element in the decree was the designation of the Protestant bodies as "Churches and ecclesial communities." The concession is a significant one. The former Catholic position was that the separation of these groups from Rome in the sixteenth century had deprived them entirely of their participation in the true Church as founded by Christ, that their individual members could indeed lead a life of grace but that the body as such was not a vehicle through which that grace flowed from Christ to its members. The teaching presented in the decree on ecumenism represents a big advance from that position. It is still somewhat vague, although the vagueness also has its ecumenical aspect. For example, the expression

"Churches and ecclesial communities" serves on the one hand to satisfy Council Fathers who did not want to call Protestant denominations Churches, but it also meets the problem of some Protestant denominations who do not want to describe themselves as Churches.

What is specific and positive, however, is the recognition of a true Christian life in these bodies as such. "Some and even most of the significant elements and endowments which together go to build up and give life to the Church itself," reads the decree, "can exist outside the visible boundaries of the Catholic Church: the written word of God; the life of grace; faith, hope, and charity, with the other interior gifts of the Holy Spirit, and visible elements too. All of these, which come from Christ and lead back to Christ, belong by right to the one Church of Christ. The brethren divided from us also use many liturgical actions of the Christian religion. These most certainly can truly engender a life of grace in ways that vary according to the condition of each Church or community. These liturgical actions must be regarded as capable of giving access to the community of salvation."

The decree, in addition, reflects an enormous advance on the subject of worship in common. Catholic practice since the Reformation has prohibited participation by Catholics in the religious services of any other denomination. It was usual to permit attendance at a ceremony for social or business reasons, such as a wedding of Protestant friends or funeral rites. However, in such cases the Catholic was admonished that his presence must remain passive, that he should not participate in the prayers. The Council stopped far short of a general approval of Catholic participation in Protestant worship. It said, nevertheless, that worship in common is a witness to the unity of the Church and a sharing in the means of grace. Insofar as it is a witness to unity, it cannot be permitted between those who in fact are not united; but insofar as it is a sharing in the means of grace, it may at times be commended. The precise extent to which it may be practiced, the Council said, should be determined by each bishop in his diocese, subject to more general rules to be laid down by national or regional conferences of bishops and by the pope.

Here, again, the reservations were intended not only to soften the impact of the change for conservative Catholics, but also to take account of the rights of the other Churches. How this might work out in practice was demonstrated in Germany soon after the decree was promulgated. In March 1965, the German Catholic bishops issued a statement authorizing a very limited participation by Catholics in common worship. Criticism by Catholics both in Germany and elsewhere was bitter. Many felt that the German bishops had talked boldly, but when it came to deeds, had suddenly drawn back. In May, however, Cardinal Jaeger, of Paderborn, had an opportunity to give an explanation at Germany's tenth ecumenical conference, an annual meeting in which Catholic and Protestant churchmen and newsmen participate. The bishops, he said, had not gone nearly as far in their March statement as they wished. They had held back out of deference to a joint statement issued by the Evangelical Church and the United Lutheran Church in January 1965, a statement that had expressed grave misgivings about church services at which a Protestant pastor and a Catholic priest both officiate. In such an atmosphere, the Catholic bishops wanted to avoid any suspicion of proselytism being attached to the Catholic ecumenical movement.

The German bishops envisaged three areas of ecumenical encounter as opened up by the Council decree. First, this called for a common effort in the social and humanitarian sphere, without toning down doctrinal differences, and with the laity in the front rank because they are generally the experts in this area. Next came co-operation in a common Christian witness to God and to the shared Christian inheritance, affirming the spiritual conception of man and the specific values of Christianity. And finally there was the area of prayer in common.

As a beginning, the bishops set up a machinery for contact with Protestant Churches at the national and state levels. The first item proposed for discussion was Baptism, the sacrament that makes one a Christian. The object here was to ensure uniformity in the manner of conferring the sacrament, thereby ending once and for all the practice of conditional Baptism when an individual joins one Christian Church from another. This was the issue that aroused strong and justified protests from many sides when President Johnson's younger daughter entered the Roman Catholic Church in 1965. Next, they proposed a common evaluation of the Christian view of marriage. A widespread result of the marriage of Christians of different denominations was a decline of Christian practice by both partners as the easy way of overcoming their differences. It is hoped instead to develop positive elements of agreement and thus to strengthen the common Christianity of the spouses without interfering with their separate beliefs.

Such beginnings can be projected into many other areas. Mixed committees could develop recommendations to eliminate unnecessary conflicts in the canon law of the various Churches, a particularly practical proposal in view of the current major revision of the Catholic Code of Canon Law. Mission authorities of the Churches need to work out methods of breaking down rivalries in their work and of giving a Christian witness through a common effort to raise the living levels of the underdeveloped countries. Closer contact between the Catholic and Protestant religious press is also envisaged, as well as a revision of catechetical texts, a common text of the Scriptures, and a common form for some church services.

Similar initiatives have also been taken in the United States, especially those touching on the problems of friendly civil coexistence, the presentation of religious news, the content of catechetical texts, and the methods of religious instruction. Work on an approved common text of the Scriptures is also moving rapidly. However, in the aspects concerning the substance of the common Christianity, we are not very much beyond the stage of lip service. Formal contacts have been established by the setting up of teams of theologians and other experts on both sides, the first meetings reflecting the American atmosphere of personal cordiality and readiness to talk.

Few American Catholics, nevertheless, believe that it is possible to go beyond the realm of co-operation as separate but friendly institutions in the sociocivic area. Most do not recognize the Christian values alive in the Churches around them which are absent from or atrophied in their own institutionalized forms. Even many educated Catholics see American Protestantism as sliding rapidly down the slope of disintegration into secularist Humanism. Rather than waste time dealing with institutions which they regard as decaying, they think they should concentrate on protecting their own from the same dangers and building their strength by luring as many non-Catholics as they can from their sinking rafts to the safety of the barque of Peter.

The institutional differences certainly cannot be minimized. It is hard to conceive today, except perhaps in France, the Low Countries, and Germany, any organic reunion of Western Christendom in which the entire Christian community in a given city, town, or village would worship together under one pastor, join in celebrating the Eucharist and in receiving the sacraments. Yet nothing less is the goal set for Catholics by Vatican II, and if many still do not understand or approve it, it nevertheless remains the goal.

And if institutional differences may not be minimized, neither should they be maximized. Even such a burning issue as the validity of Anglican orders, an issue clouding relations between Roman Catholics and Episcopalians in the United States, is not so closed as Catholics have long imagined. Rome decided in 1896 that Anglican Orders were defective because of a break in apostolic succession in the consecration of bishops at the time of Cranmer in the sixteenth century. Today, however, that decision is not regarded by all Catholic theologians as irreversible.

A further important dimension of the issue is often overlooked. The Orders of the Episcopal Church of Scotland and of the Church of Ireland are not in the same historical category as those of the Church of England. The Church of Ireland, for example, was formally reintegrated into communion with Rome a century after Cranmer's death by Papal Nuncio Rinuccini, when the Roman Catholics and the Reformed Church united in opposition to Cromwell. In addition, after Rome's nineteenth-century decree, Orthodox and Old Catholic bishops often joined as coconsecrators of bishops of the Anglican Church, and there has always been intercommunion and coconsecration of bishops by the Anglican Church and the Episcopal Churches of Scotland and Ireland. The total effect of all these relations is to create a high degree of probability of valid consecration of Anglican bishops today, even assuming that Rome's nineteenth-century decision on Anglican Orders was final.

Vatican II did not become involved in this issue. While it clearly affirmed in the decree on ecumenism the validity of Orthodox Orders, it was deliberately vague regarding those of the Reformed Churches. Its one reference is to the "ecclesial communities," that is to say, the Christian groups who do not regard themselves as "Churches" and either deny or are vague about a special priesthood transmitted by the sacrament of Orders. Catholics, it says, do not believe that such communities have retained "the proper reality of the Eucharistic mystery in its fullness." Yet even in these cases, the decree adds, by commemorating the death and resurrection of Christ in the Lord's Supper, "they profess that it signifies life in communion with Christ and look forward to His coming in glory."

Another confrontation within the Council that began by threatening ecumenical relations but ended by boosting them considerably occurred during the discussion of the decree on revelation. As originally presented at the first session in 1962, the document revived one of the basic issues over which the Reformers split with Rome. Drawn up in a strictly polemical framework, it was entitled "The Sources of Revelation." For Protestants, all revealed truth is contained in the Scriptures. Catholics since Trent have tended to treat Tradition as a separate and perhaps more important source.

The debate played a major part in establishing the theological conscience of the Council. It quickly emerged that something deeper than two viewpoints regarding a specific theological thesis was at stake. The conflict actually began with the distinct idea that each side had of religious knowledge. One group of Fathers was quite at home with the precise definitions of the seminary manuals, which left no room for new intellectual acquisitions resulting from dialogue with others. For them, everything was defined, classified, and tied to proofs. History had little to tell them. Others had already drawn from the Scriptures and from the Fathers of the Church all they had to contribute, and their task was restricted to raising the ivory tower ever higher on the bases contributed by earlier theologians.

The majority and finally the Council itself challenged this approach. Rejecting by a vote of 1,368 to 822 the treatment based on pure rationality, it affirmed the strictly religious nature of knowledge of God's revelation. Pope John approved of its decisions and cut through the red tape of Council regulations to withdraw the offending draft and call for a new start.

The redrafted document as finally approved skirted the issue on which the other had foundered. It presented Scripture and Tradition, not as two sources but rather as two complementary channels through which is transmitted a single divine revelation to man. It said that Tradition is wider than Scripture, but only in the sense that the ultimate certitude about the meaning of all that is revealed in the Scriptures cannot be drawn from the Scriptures themselves. Its position was that the life of the Church, or Tradition, gives this certitude, a position similar to that reached by the Faith and Order Conference of the World Council of Churches at Montreal, Canada, in 1963. It got away from legalistic formulations of revelation as a series of prescriptions, stressing instead the concept of a body of words and acts, the person of Jesus as savior of man. Revelation, it indicated, is not a body of formal propositions, like one of the mathematical sciences, but a guide to living. And it is the final rule of faith, to which the teaching authority in the Church is subject. This would seem a truth so obvious as to be tautological. Nevertheless, the stress of post-Reformation Catholic theologians on the authority of the earthly and institutional Church has distracted attention from the transcendence of Christ, tending to present the pope as a king in his own right and not simply as the vicar of Christ. Catholic apologists were reluctant to state unambiguously that the pope remains at all times subject to the objective rule of revelation. The Council did so.

Also of great satisfaction to the Protestants was the clarification by the decree of the meaning of inspiration and inerrancy in the Scriptures. At an earlier time, it was the Protestants who most insisted on a literal interpretation of every word and sentence in the Scriptures as immediately dictated by God and consequently to be taken as true in every respect. The development of historical and critical sciences long ago established that such literalism was not intellectually defensible. Protestant scholars led the way in these sciences, and Catholics tended to hold back, even when individual scholars saw the untenability of the old positions. Pope Pius XII opened up new ground in encyclicals written in 1943 and 1951, but conservatives entrenched in the regulatory organs of the Roman Curia whittled down the concessions made by Pius to such an extent that Catholic scholars remained subject to arbitrary vexations.

All this has now changed. While reaffirming that the Scriptures are truly and fully the word of God, teaching divine truth without error, the Council approved a full and objective evaluation of the historical, literary, and scientific realities. It acknowledged that there is no absolute way to interpret the Scriptures, that the Church in each age, under the inspiration of the Holy Spirit and in keeping with the intellectual progress of mankind, can gain more meaningful appreciation of the mysteries of divine revelation in relation to the facts of salvation, as achieved by Christ in His birth, death, and resurrection.

Finally, a constant and justified Protestant criticism of Roman Catholic practice was faced by the Council. Even before the Reformation, little effort was made to encourage the Catholic people to read the Scriptures or even to make available versions they could read. With the stress of the Reformers on the Scriptures as the rule of faith, the Catholic Church actively discouraged the reading of the Scriptures. Approved translations have become more available in modern times, but little effort was made to popularize their use.

The first draft of the decree on revelation was guarded in its approach to private reading of the Scriptures. It seemed to suggest that it was proper only for priests. The final version corrected this holdover from the polemics of the Counter Reformation. "Let all the faithful," it said, "come to an outstanding knowledge of Jesus Christ by the contant reading of the Scriptures." In addition, resolving yet another polemical issue, it recommended the widest distribution of translations of the Scriptures.

Yet after all this is said, it must be recognized that the remaining issues between Rome and other Western Christians are immense. Deep theological differences, even with the most favorable atmosphere on both sides, will take a long time to identify clearly, to say nothing of resolving. But such an atmosphere is still far from being achieved.

Many Protestants consequently share the Orthodox view expressed earlier. The Catholic mind, they believe, still remains in imperial, legalistic, and self-sufficient molds. The issue came into the open in the last days of the third session of the Council in November, 1964. During the so-called Black Week, many things conspired to cause dismay to ecumenists, the two most pertinent here being the explanatory note added to the decree on the nature of the Church and the changes inserted in the decree on ecumenism.

In his opening speech to that session, Pope Paul had referred to the issue of collegiality as "the weightiest and most delicate" problem before the Council, while indicating his own approval of the doctrine and his hope that the Fathers would vote it during the session. Yet, a little earlier, in the encyclical *Ecclesiam suam,* he had warned that he reserved to himself the choice of the proper moment and manner of expressing his judgment, which he hoped would be in accord with that of the Council Fathers. He was insisting on an issue on which there was no dispute in the Council, and doing so in a way that seemed to envisage the possibility of conflict between two distinct sources of supreme authority in the Church, the college consisting of the bishops with the pope, and the pope acting by himself independently of the college.

This formulation caused no little dismay among Protestant observers. They found themselves confronted with the legalistic and casuistic box from which they hoped the Catholic Church had escaped. Their shock was increased both by the content of the "explanatory note," which highlights the same distinction, and by the way it was presented to the Council. There was no opportunity for debate and little for informal exchange of views. At the last moment, the Fathers were handed what they were given to understand was an official papal interpretation of the document. All that went on the record was that it was transmitted "by higher authority," but it was universally understood that it was, in fact, the pope's own decision. The only choice left to the Fathers was to reject the entire document because of an "explanatory note" that they were assured did not alter its theological sense, or bow humbly to the inevitable. A few days later, they had to repeat the experience when the decree on ecumenism came up for final vote with 19 changes "introduced by higher authority and accepted by the Secretariat for Unity," in the words of General Secretary Felici to the Fathers.

Some of these changes were important to the ecumenists.

The text approved earlier the same month, with about 2,000 Fathers in favor in each of a series of votes and no more than 85 opposed, said that non-Catholic Christians *are* followers of Christ. The modified text said they *profess to be* followers of Christ. The earlier text, which said they *find* God in the Scriptures, was changed to *they seek*. The statement that their finding of God in the Scriptures resulted from the action of the Holy Spirit was further modified to say that they *invoke* the Holy Spirit while seeking God in the Scriptures. And an additional change in the same sentence cast further doubt on the result of their search for God while invoking the Holy Spirit. The text approved by the Fathers said that God spoke to them in Christ. The altered version presented God "as it were speaking to them in Christ." What the phrase does mean is not clear. But when it is compared with what was in the earlier text, it is clear that it tends to weaken and hedge.

The earlier text said that the Eastern Churches had the *right and duty* to govern themselves, which was modified to read that they are *authorized* to do so. The earlier text said that some Orthodox Churches *are* apostolic in origin, which was changed to read that they *proudly claim* to have such an origin. And where the earlier text said that the gifts of the Spirit can be found among other Christians, the revision recognizes only "the riches of Christ and virtuous works in the lives of others who are bearing witness to Christ."

Again the experts agree that the text is not altered substantially and that the new wording does not exclude the truth of the earlier statements but simply does not affirm it. However, taken as a group, all the changes express a spirit hostile to the positions of the Protestants, and they were in fact regarded by the most friendly and understanding of the Protestant observers at the Council as offensive to them and harmful to the ecumenical movement. Their chagrin and embarrassment were multiplied when the pope chose the closing ceremony of the session to proclaim Mary "Mother of the Church." The proposal had been debated at length in the chapter on Mary in the decree on the Church, and the Fathers had decided not to introduce this title, in part because of disagreements regarding its basis in tradition, in part because of the difficulties it would create both for the Orthodox and for the Protestants. When, on

November 18, the pope indicated his intention of proclaiming Mary as Mother of the Church, it was understood that the ceremony would take place on the afternoon of November 21 at St. Mary Major, making it possible for the Orthodox and Protestant observers at the Council to stay away. Instead, the pope devoted a large part of his closing address to the topic.

"A bad blow to ecumenism and a shock to Protestants," was the reaction of Robert McAfee Brown, commenting on the total impact of this series of events during the final week of the session. Council expert Father Yves Congar agreed. "The psychological harm done on the ecumenical level is infinitely regrettable," he said. In a joint press conference, three of the Protestant observers deplored the pope's action. The changes in the ecumenism decree, said Dr. H. A. Oberman, of the Harvard Divinity School, had the effect of stating that the Protestants do not belong to Christ's Church and have nothing of Christ in their communion services. Professor L. J. van Holk added that Pope Paul's recent warning about modernistic and Protestant tendencies showed a misconception of the place of Protestants in the modern world. Finally, Professor P. J. Maan said that despite the establishment of the principle of collegiality, the pope in his actions did not appear to acknowledge such sharing of authority.

The total effect was to confirm once more a deep-rooted Protestant suspicion of Rome, an attitude that has little to do with theological differences and much to do with cultural predispositions. The issue has been very well presented by Hans Küng in one of his earlier books on the Council.[7] He quotes the Protestant theologian Karl Barth as saying in his book *Church Dogmatics* that the difference between Catholics and Protestants on the subject of apostolic succession is not concerned with the fact but with the manner. And even as regards the manner, Barth has no protest in principle against the Catholic belief that the summation of the apostolate was in Peter, or even that Christ might have established a primacy in the Church and accorded it to the Roman community. So far Barth's presentation of the problem in his book. But, adds Küng, Barth went farther in conversation: "I cannot," he said, "hear the voice of the Good Shepherd as coming from this 'chair of Peter.'"

[7] *The Council in Action* (New York, Sheed & Ward, 1963).

Yet another continuing obstacle to ecumenism is the Roman determination to maintain Scholastic philosophy as the sole vehicle through which to express theological viewpoints and revealed truth. The issue was brought home to the Fathers by the issuance of an encyclical by Pope Paul as they assembled for the final session of the Council. Entitled *Mysterium fidei*, it dealt with the teaching of the Church regarding the Holy Eucharist and the respect to be paid to the consecrated host. There was indeed no new teaching in this encyclical, but some Italian newspapers built it up into a sensation. The pope, they claimed, was reprimanding the Dutch bishops for their failure to curb certain discussions in the Netherlands on the subject.

It is noteworthy that this misinterpretation appeared on the same day in *Il Tempo*, an outlet for the views of the intransigent sectors of the Curia, and in the Communist daily *Unità*. The fact was that less than two months earlier, the pope had written Cardinal Alfrink to congratulate the entire Dutch hierarchy on the prudent way they had dealt with the issue in a joint pastoral letter. The pastoral letter had approved of the open discussion taking place in the Netherlands of problems raised by modern philosophies concerning the Eucharist, while reserving judgment on extreme views expressed by some of the discussants.

Actually, the principal point at issue is not the reality of the presence of Christ in the Eucharist, which Trent had defined as a change of the substance of the bread and wine into the substance of the body and blood of Christ. It concerns the way of conceiving of the substance of the bread and wine, the definition of substance rather than the reality of transubstantiation. The problem is a serious one. In the era of atomic science, with its extraordinarily expanded knowledge of the elements of which the material world is composed, few take the Scholastic concepts of substance and accident and of matter and form any more seriously than they would take the cosmogony of the ancient Greeks.

The issues that may be raised by the definitions of Trent presumably would fall into the same category as historical inaccuracies in the Scriptures, subject to the same explanation as that offered by Vatican II for the inerrancy of the Scriptures. It certainly seems legitimate to ask if the inerrancy of the Church's definitions must be of a higher kind than that of the

Scriptures. If the latter can and do teach divine truth without error, even when the authors present as a historical truth something that is not such, then it would seem that the same criterion could be applied to the teaching of Councils. But this would threaten the privileged sanctuary in which Scholasticism had been enshrined. Rome is not yet ready for that.

Such reactions explain the insistence of many leading ecumenists that common action by the Churches and a gradual widening of the realm of worship in common must precede any serious progress toward corporate unity of Catholics and other Christians. They encourage the widest and frankest discussions by theologians to isolate and define issues. But they believe that emotional understanding must precede and inspire intellectual agreement.

In this context, the ecumenical service held in the Basilica of St. Paul in Rome on one of the last days of the Council assumes special meaning. Here, Pope Paul and the Catholic bishops joined with the Orthodox, Protestant, and Anglican observers at the Council in readings from the Scriptures, hymns, psalms, and liturgical texts. The pope himself led the service and preached a sermon in which he insisted on the communion that already exists among all Christians in spite of division on specific points of doctrine or practice. That the worship was fully common was stressed by the fact that the passages were read alternatively by Catholics and members of the other Churches.

Many examples also exist of the possibilities of common action open to Christians as a result of the texts and spirit of the Council. The most logical of all is co-operation in making texts of the Scriptures universally available and encouraging all Christians to read them regularly. The preliminary step of agreeing on a common version is being taken in many countries, including the United States. The Protestant monks of Taizé, France, pioneers of ecumenism since their foundation in 1940, give this work the highest priority. During the Council, they established close relations with many bishops from Latin America and developed a series of programs to help the development of that region. This includes a project to distribute a million copies of an agreed text of the New Testament.

Most of the Taizé programs in Latin America are in the

social, cultural, educational, and humanitarian fields, and these are areas in which immediate ecumenical co-operation is particularly needed. Christians in recent times have become more ready to help each other in times of disaster or acute emergency, but are still reluctant to merge educational and charitable institutions. However, significant initiatives have taken place since the start of the Council, such as the exchange of students between Catholic seminaries and those of other denominations, and even the merging of theological faculties.

Nowhere is the need for pooling of material resources and personnel more urgent than in the mission countries of the underdeveloped world. Those involved in mission work had long been saddened by the scandal of a Christianity that presented itself to non-Christians as divided in its teachings and negating its proclamation of brotherly love by its competing institutions. The Council gave the mission-minded an opportunity to project their concerns to a much wider audience. It was a sympathetic audience, but its members reflected many interests and backgrounds. Even those who agreed fully in principle on the need to co-operate were often shocked to find that Christian mission co-operation did not simply mean the adding together of the personnel, funds, and institutions that formerly functioned separately or, perhaps, competitively. It required a more basic evaluation of the principles on which many of the institutions themselves had been based, a subject so far-reaching as to merit a separate chapter.

Chapter 6

Blessed
Are the Poor

Poverty is a problem with which men have wrestled not only from the foundation of Christianity but from the beginnings of human society. Man cannot live without material things, yet he always tends to be enslaved by them. Jesus said, "Blessed are the poor in spirit," but there are few sermons on poverty in the United States; if they were delivered, what would they mean to a typical congregation?

The scandal of world hunger is more terrible than ever before, since it is only in this century that the technical means have become available to eliminate the degradation of sub-human living. As for the Church, it never before devoted such immense resources to the direct relief of poverty and the illnesses caused by poverty throughout the world, as well as to their indirect relief, by sending teachers and technical experts to mission lands. Yet never before have wealth and the appearance of wealth formed such a barrier between the Church and its mission. Great masses of the poor feel themselves alienated from a Church that lives in comfort. Many see it as a parasite, an ally of rich individuals and nations seeking to retain for themselves an excessive part of the world's wealth.

Many within the Church have long been aware of these attitudes and have recognized the validity of the criticism without knowing what their response should be. One could reasonably argue that the Church is not a Church *of* the poor. Christians tend to belong to the more comfortable districts of a town, to the better-off class of a country, to the more wealthy continents of the world. In countries of traditional Catholicism, the Church has traditionally seen itself as a Church *for* the poor. Thanks to the support of the state, itself controlled by the Church's wealthy members, it has been able to serve the poor through charitable and educational institutions, to impose on them a degree of religious belief and practice, and to drill them in the civic virtues conducive to the stability of society.

In the United States the issue was posed somewhat differently but not less acutely. Separation of church and state had allowed the Catholic Church to identify with the poor during its formative period. By the twentieth century, nevertheless, the Church had risen with them to a level of material comfort which in the United States represented only middle-class normality, but in world terms ranged American Catholicism on the side of privilege and power. At home, it had nothing to say to the Negro, the sharecropper, the slum dweller. Abroad, many saw its function as the serving of the nation's world interests by keeping the destitute from desperation with crumbs scattered from its rich table.

The question bishops had to ask themselves was whether it was proper to jeopardize their relations with their comfortable flocks in order to win the support of the poor in the new social situation of the twentieth century. It might not even be enough to espouse the way of life and the culture of the poor. In the many countries in which the rich and the poor are in a state of virtual war, the Church would have to embrace the cause of the poor, their destiny, their struggle for life.

For a century, up to the time of Pope John, a succession of popes had answered the question in the same way. Their social teaching had steadily enlarged the claims of the workers, of the poor, but the popes had all thought of themselves and of the Church as allied with the state in conferring benefits on the masses. John was the first to reject this position. As historian E. E. Y. Hales observes, he was less concerned than his predecessors, in the political sense, with saving the position of the Church. "He was largely free from the Counter Reformation habit of using politics as a weapon of defense against heresy, from the Renaissance habit of using politics to strengthen the papal position in Italy, and from the medieval habit of using politics to build a papal ascendancy over Europe."[1] John refused to discriminate among people on the basis of what they could do for him or for the Church. Each individual was equal in personal dignity and had, accordingly, an equal claim on the pope as a father and on the Church as a mother.

The statement on poverty made by John in September 1962, a month before the Council opened, was fully in keeping with this attitude. "A guiding light for the Council must be this," he said, "that with regard to the underdeveloped countries, the Church is to show herself as the Church of all men, and above all as the Church of the poor. Our Lord himself taught us that the poor will have the first places in the kingdom of God. The society of Christ on earth must therefore be based less on the possession of worldly goods than on renunciation and poverty. The spirit of the Gospel is thus reflected in the Church of the poor."

When the Council began to discuss the nature of the Church, many bishops recalled Pope John's observations on poverty. Christianity's oldest and deepest traditions, they said, everywhere stressed Christ's special regard in word and act for the poor. The Council should not overlook this aspect of the Church's nature.

The suggestion was immediately echoed by many of the Fathers, though for a variety of reasons, according to the situation of each. Those living in the mission territories of Asia and Africa, in the Near East, the Moslem world, and Latin America saw the practical advantage for themselves of a statement proclaiming a deep concern of the Church for its poor. Combined with collegiality, which included the notion of a universal concern of each part of the Church for every other part, it would encourage a more equal distribution of the Church's human and material resources for the benefit of the poorer regions.

"There is in the world today a vast army of men, women and children gathered under the banner of misery and poverty," in the words of Bishop Georges Mercier of the Sahara. "Out of three billion human beings, two billion belong to this army, and they are on the verge of revolt. The situation in the world

[1] *Pope John and His Revolution* (New York, Doubleday & Co., 1965).

is as grave as that. The Council has raised great hopes in the breasts of the wretched ones of the world, and many bishops realize with anguish that if, in fact, the Council achieves nothing to repair the enormous scandal of the inequality of man and man, the whole thing may well be regarded by the majority of mankind as a bitter disappointment."[2]

Bishops living under Communist regimes were anxious for a Council statement on poverty, although for a different reason. Official propaganda in their countries presents religion as an ally of capitalism in oppressing the poor. They would welcome words and actions by the Church, calculated to blunt the force of that argument. Priests, religious, and especially bishops should not own real estate, Bishop Franjo Franič of Yugoslavia told the Council. They should get rid of "land holdings which they do not work with their own hands, and all buildings in which they do not live and which do not serve for apostolic purposes, and in general all material goods which without work bring gain according to the capitalistic system." Clergy and religious, he said, "should live from their own apostolic work, like St. Peter, or from their own physical work, like St. Paul, or from the spontaneous offerings of the faithful."

Bishop Franič and his colleagues further wanted a clarification of Catholic teaching on the economic aspects of current political systems. Were Catholics obliged, for example, to reject the Communist economic system because it insisted on public ownership of the means of production?

The Council did in fact throw some light on this point. Because of an error that had crept into Leo XIII's encyclical on the rights of workers issued in 1891, Catholic theologians and sociologists of the first half of the twentieth century had tended to be unduly intransigent about private property. *Rerum novarum* had described private property as a divinely decreed right, and they concluded that the Communist economic system could not be reconciled with Catholic teaching.

In its statement on the Church in the Modern World, the Council spelled out at some length a correction of the mistake made in *Rerum novarum*, a mistake to which Popes Pius XII and John XXIII had adverted in official documents. St. Thomas

[2] From an interview given to the Information Service of the White Fathers, the text of which was released in Rome on October 8, 1963.

Aquinas had not taught, as the drafters of *Rerum novarum* believed, that private property was a divinely decreed right. What he had said was that mankind had a divine right to use all the material goods of the universe for its benefit. Private property was a method, though not necessarily the only one, to implement this purpose.

The Council, accordingly, carefully limited itself to asserting, in the statement on the Church in the Modern World, a modest right to "some ownership of external goods" as "wholly necessary for the autonomy of the person and the family" and as "an extension of human freedom." It quickly added that this right was not opposed to public ownership, including expropriation (subject to fair compensation) in the public interest, and that public authority was entitled to prevent abuse of private property to the detriment of the common good, since "by its very nature private property has a social quality which is based on the law of the common destination of earthly goods."

During the early years of the Council, these same issues had become of immediate practical importance to bishops far removed from Communist lands. The newly independent governments of Africa, for example, had begun to preach something they called African Socialism, a nondoctrinaire approach to public control of the major means of production that seemed much closer in practice to the Communist economic system than to that of the West. Some bishops found no difficulty in accepting such economic trends. The hierarchy of Kenya in the middle of 1965, while the statement on the Church in the Modern World was still being written, explicitly approved the government's espousal of African Socialism as national policy.

From very early in the Council, many had felt that the opportunity for an exchange of views on this subject by bishops from all over the world should not be missed. During the first session, accordingly, a study group was formed by interested Fathers to attempt to analyze opinion and formulate practical suggestions. Its leaders included Cardinal Gerlier of France and Cardinal Lercaro of Italy, Archbishop Helder Camara and Bishop Mercier. Strangely enough, this Church-of-the-Poor group did not include a single representative of the hierarchies of any of the Anglo-Saxon countries. Some bishops from these wealthy countries seemed to regard the group as designed to rebuke them for living affluently, or as a pressure apparatus created for the purpose of extracting from them a higher level of aid for the missions.

The study group succeeded in gradually crystallizing some basic issues. "One fact that stands out," according to French Bishop Alfred Ancel, a member of the group, "is that in many countries the Church appears to the poor as a stranger, even as an enemy. They believe it is rich and powerful, linked to the wealthy and to the power structures." The Church was urged in particular to face up to the challenge of Marxism, not because Marxism had the right answers but because it asked the right questions. Christians were also chided for having come belatedly and often reluctantly to the support of industrial and domestic workers, leaving the initiative in this Christlike work to philosophers and the labor movement.

Few, if any, were prepared to challenge the validity of such criticisms. Many, nevertheless, were unwilling to meditate on them or project them to logical conclusions. Those who attempted to do so recognized that they could have an impact on Church organization more profound than that of the principle of collegiality written into the statement on the nature of the Church. An immediate effect would be to shatter the Vatican wealth and power structures, with significant implications for the Italian economy and the political balance of power between the Left and Right in Italy.

Vatican finances have been one of the most sacred of the Church's sacred cows. For a long time, nevertheless, they have been openly criticized in Europe's anticlerical press. More recently, the new climate of freedom of expression has permitted cautious comment in Catholic publications and open discussion in the general press. The discussion, it is true, has been handicapped by the Vatican's refusal to participate. But if Vatican secretiveness obscures details, it no more hides the major facts than the secrecy attempted at the Council's first session kept from the world what was going on.

A major distinction—made by all responsible commentators —is between revenue-producing wealth and that which of its nature does not produce income in a Capitalist society. The latter includes the world's most valuable art collection—priceless treasures buried in the Vatican palaces and in extraterritorial papal properties in Rome, Loreto, Assisi, and Padua.

Also to be excluded from the calculation, or rather to be evaluated differently, are the hundreds of churches in the city of Rome. The number is out of all proportion to pastoral needs. One often finds three or four in a single block. And the number grows as new religious congregations seek to build up their status by erecting a central house and church as imposing as the next.

Also to be excluded from a determination of Vatican finances, although not from an evaluation of the Church as seen by the world's poor, are the immense properties of innumerable ecclesiastical bodies—dioceses, religious orders, colleges, and charitable institutions. Legal ownership varies from country to country according to law and custom, but the properties are not directly owned by the Vatican, nor does the Vatican normally have a significant voice in the routine management and disposition of properties and funds.

Having properly put to one side all this Church wealth, *The Economist* (London, March 1965) estimates that Vatican investments in securities quoted on the stock exchanges of the world totaled in 1965 not less than $5.6 billion, perhaps considerably more. This, it says, makes the Vatican "an international financial power of formidable size." Its realizable assets would be about equal to the official gold and foreign reserves of France, five times the dollar securities held by the British government, exceeded as investment portfolios only by the largest American mutual life insurance companies.

Nor does this investment portfolio, notes *The Economist*, represent the total business wealth of the Vatican. It owns real estate and land in numerous European countries and in North and South America. It is a major landlord in Rome, with blocks of houses and apartments as well as big stretches of land on the outskirts of the city. The mere fact of such ownership encourages rumors of involvement in political deals. The Leftist publication *L'Expresso*, for example, charged that the Via Olimpica in Rome was routed to favor Vatican real estate interests, increasing the value of properties of Church-related organizations from 30 billion lire to 55 billion. And a more moderate observer had this to say: "In Italy, the man in the street who pays his monthly gas, electric, telephone, and water bills to companies in which the Vatican holds shares, and from time to time interest on his loan from the Bank of the Holy Spirit, is understandably irked by the whole business." The bizarrely named bank is a Vatican-controlled commercial bank doing business in Italy.

Most of the Vatican's portfolio investments are outside Italy. *The Economist* puts the Italian share at less than one-tenth. It is, however, the part that in recent years has made headlines. In late 1962, a Center-Left government in Italy imposed a withholding tax on dividends, as most developed countries now do. The law provided for exemption for citizens of other states, by bilateral agreement. The Vatican claimed this exemption, and the Italian treasury sent a confidential circular to the companies affected, authorizing them to pay dividends to the Vatican without withholding taxes.

When, shortly after, a Socialist became finance minister and learned about the arrangement, he insisted that the Parliament should approve. In the subsequent negotiations, unofficial estimates were made of Vatican holdings of Italian shares, estimates on which the Italian government and the Vatican seemed in agreement. According to them, the Vatican owns about one-fifteenth of all shares quoted on Italian stock exchanges, giving it a stake of at least $560 million in Italian enterprises in 1965.

Vatican interlocking of interests with and influence on the Italian economy showed up most clearly under Pius XII. Count Enrico Galeazzi, Knight of the Grand Cross, Secret Chamberlain of the Sword and Cape, simultaneously headed the Vatican City administration and was vice-president of the Board of Directors of Generale Immobiliare, Italy's giant real estate trust, and on the board of directors of half a dozen of Italy's biggest companies. The three Pacelli princes and other Vatican notables also figured prominently in the directorates of leading companies.

Pope John downgraded Galeazzi and his colleagues by giving final control of financial policy to two cardinals, Cicognani and Di Jorio. They still retain no small importance, however. Galeazzi had 8 entries in the 1965 *Annuario Pontificio*, official Vatican yearbook, as compared with 1 for most bishops, 9 for Cardinal Cushing of Boston, and 13 for Cardinal Spellman of

New York. His jobs included that of special delegate of the Papal Commission for Vatican City State and director general of the Office of Technical Services and the Office of Economic Services. An architect by profession, he was also a member of the Administrative Secretariat of the Council and on the postconciliar Commission for the Communications Media.

Cash for Vatican investments has been accumulated in many ways. An important source was Mussolini's payment, under the Lateran Treaty of 1929, of 1.5 billion lire (then worth 83 million dollars) in settlement of Vatican claims for the properties Italy had seized in 1870. Inspired administration, combined with the Vatican's world-wide sources of information and freedom from currency controls and taxes has snowballed the capital value of the Lateran Treaty fund. Corrado Pallenberg, author of *Inside the Vatican,* makes an educated guess that by 1960 it had grown to 500 million dollars. Additional funds come from the annual world-wide collection known as "Peter's Pence," from collections for Propagation of the Faith and the Holy Childhood associations, and from administration of properties held by the Holy See before 1870 or subsequently donated to it. Some of these funds are handled by the "Institute for Religious Works," a Vatican bank founded by Pope Pius XII and staffed mainly by clerics. It does business all over the world, much of it on behalf of religious orders. Advantages include freedom from government financial restrictions and complete secrecy.

Few would deny the usefulness of working capital to maintain the Church's world-wide network of religious, social, and charitable organizations, especially in mission lands. What is questioned is the need for a financial empire of the present proportions and the use to which much of the income is put. Is the proclaimed Christian spirit of poverty advanced by cardinals who drive around Rome in chauffered limousines with diplomatic plates, maintaining the style of ambassadors of world powers, when ordinary Romans are happy to have a scooter or tiny car? How edified is one who passes through the world's most foul-smelling slum in the city of Karachi, Pakistan, to reach the fabulous palace newly constructed for the apostolic internuncio on a headland sweetened by sea breezes? Nor is

Karachi the only city in which the palaces of the Church of the Poor cause scandal.

In addition to the bad impression on the observer, vested interests affect the outlook of churchmen. "If I have shares on the stock exchange," one bishop commented during the Council, "and watch the daily reports for the rise and fall of their value, I shall inevitably hesitate to make a decision that may adversely affect the market, even if the action would be good for the Church."

What seems most immediately necessary is a public accounting. "Is it not time," wrote Otto B. Roegele, Professor at Munich University and editor of the *Rheinischer Merkur*, in March 1965, "to lift the veil of secrecy from the Vatican finances? . . . The twilight in which rumors flourish may have been bearable in the era of absolutism of the princes of the Church, but today it can only be harmful to the Church's reputation."

The issue is not restricted to the Vatican. It affects the Catholic Church throughout the world, and the Council discussed it and made Catholics discuss it in those terms. There was, for example, widespread criticism of the approach of the Catholic Relief Services of the bishops of the United States. Since World War II this organization has performed a unique service of emergency feeding of the poor in many parts of the world. Many feel, however, that it tends to institutionalize poverty by stressing the distribution of surplus food from the United States more than the building up of the productive capacity, agricultural and industrial, of the areas it serves. The fact that nearly all the relief it distributes is donated by the United States government under programs for disposing of agricultural surpluses causes many, especially in Africa, to see it as an arm of United States world policy, a cold-war weapon. "You proclaim separation of church and state," one archbishop commented bitterly, "but your bishops seem very happy to serve the State Department." Others deplore the unecumenical way in which the Catholic agency and those of other Christian denominations compete in non-Christian lands. Catholics and Mennonites, for example, have separate if equal administrations side by side in Saigon.

Other parts of the Church have their own problems caused by wealth or its appearances. One of the more bizarre was presented to the writer by Bishop Charles Brown, of Santa Cruz, Bolivia. "We have parishes and sanctuaries of the Virgin Mary which from time immemorial own thousands of acres around them," he said. "Everyone knows that such is the case. Everyone knows that they are Church property. But is it so? The land is occupied and tilled by peasants whose ancestors have always lived there. They pay no rent either in money or kind. In consequence, the Church gets no benefit from the holdings. And what is worse, it cannot get rid of them. There are no titles. So the public goes on thinking that the Church is wealthy through its extensive land holdings, feels no obligation to contribute to its support."

Taking a broader view, there is no country in which the Church's display of wealth is not an obstacle to its mission. At the Council, one Father after another railed at the baroque vestments and ornaments of the liturgy, the display of un-evangelical pomp at the very meetings of the Council, the proliferation of ridiculous titles.

Archbishop Helder Camara of Brazil started a movement to have bishops substitute a plain wooden cross, like the one he himself wears, for the jewel-studded crosses of gold that now adorn them. Pope Paul made a gesture in this direction when in November 1964 he laid his tiara on the altar of St. Peter's as a symbolic gift to the poor. Some bishops called for a basket to be passed among the bishops so that they could deposit their jeweled rings. The curialists firmly squashed the idea. The word was passed that any bishop who wished to follow the pope's lead should do so by contributing cash.

Even the tiara gesture ended in an anticlimax. The curialists insisted that the tiara, being a "sacred" object, could not be sold. It was given to Cardinal Spellman of New York as a gift for the American people, without any explanation of the logic that selected them as the poorest of the world's poor. And "informed Vatican sources" leaked the news that, despite his gift, the pope had not abandoned the practice of wearing a tiara.

The issues of wealth and poverty are similarly agitating the religious orders. One of the original features of monastic life as practiced in the Church from early times was a commitment to evangelical poverty. Like Christ's first disciples, the monks

left their homes and gave up their property and means of liveli-
hood so that they could live free from worldly preoccupations.
The original concept, however, was gradually overshadowed
by narrow legalistic interpretations. The vow of poverty, it was
argued, bound the individual monk or nun, not the religious
community. The individual was obligated to use the community goods in dependence on a superior who determined
what quantity and quality of food, clothing, equipment, cam-
eras, typewriters, tape recorders, or whatever were needed by
each to perform his function in the community.

Applying this principle, life in most convents and monasteries has evolved in step with the social and economic development of the West. The religious orders, in consequence,
no longer give a manifest evidence of evangelical poverty, even
in rich countries. They often are making impressive contributions to education, to health, to welfare, to research. But they
do not automatically evoke the poverty of Christ to which they
had voluntarily committed themselves. On the contrary, the
man in the street who sees their fine homes, their spacious
parks, their tree-lined avenues, their expensive if archaic dress,
says to himself that it's a good racket. As the Rome taxi driver
who left the writer at the central house of a religious congregation in a swank suburb commented, "The monks always do
themselves well."

The contradiction between profession and reality is visible
not only to cab drivers but to responsible members of the communities involved. "We are more sure of the next meal than
anyone else in the world," is how Father G. M. Lalande,
Superior General of the Congregation of Holy Cross, puts it.
"Some bursars and some superiors have financial worries, but
most religious are altogether free of them. And, without even
being aware of it, we have become used to a high standard of
living."[3]

The contrast becomes more extreme when priests and nuns
make the additional sacrifice of leaving friends and homeland
to work in underdeveloped countries. What for them are primitive and heroic living conditions nevertheless leave them far

[3] Quoted in Desmond O'Grady, *Eat From God's Hand* (London,
Geoffrey Chapman, 1965), p. 154.

above the poverty-stricken and starving masses. Those to whom they minister can see them only as part of a wealth and power structure in which the poor do not share and to which they cannot even aspire.

Bishop Peter A. Kobayashi, of Sendai, Japan, has reflected on the extreme contrast of wealth and poverty that forces the missionary to select the class to which he offers the good news of Christ: "It is difficult to keep track of the number of religious congregations which compete with each other for locations in such big centers as Tokyo, Yokohama, and Osaka, investing in their houses and activities huge sums of money brought from abroad. No sooner have they completed the erection of immense establishments, of which modern architecture may be proud, than they experience a mass assault from the sons and daughters of the best families, attracted by the atmosphere of money and middle-class taste. If then 1,600 candidates sit for the entrance examination for a class of 300, it certainly would seem to the casual observer that you have clear proof of the success of your efforts. Nevertheless, it is no longer permissible to entertain—as you do—this simple illusion based on ignorance. The fact is that in these same cities in which you live, there are millions and tens of millions of miserable people who have no contact with your schools. In the light of the appearances just described, these unfortunate people are quite right to regard the Catholic Church as made for the rich, to see it in the service of the Capitalists. And it terrifies me to contemplate what may be one day the consequences of this judgment."[4]

The same idea was expressed forcibly by Father Paul Gauthier, a worker-priest at Nazareth and an ardent member of the Church-of-the-Poor group at the Council. When he first went to the Holy Land, he was shocked at the gulf separating the Christian missionaries from the poor. Some of the missionaries were also distressed by the situation but did not know how to correct it. "We are on the wrong track," one of them told him. "We live in fine buildings, while the people don't even have houses. We barely talk their language. We look like foreigners, protected and subsidized by foreign nations. We are

[4] Quoted in *Informations Catholiques Internationales* (February 15, 1964).

divided among ourselves; each rite criticizes and despises the other rites. We have mistaken our path through lack of poverty and charity."[5]

Pope Paul agrees that religious orders should be more concerned about the appearance of poverty, as a sign to the world. Addressing the heads of various orders and congregations in 1964, he said that in addition to the poverty appropriate to the life of each member, poverty should shine forth from the institute itself. "In consequence, religious institutes should avoid undue elegance in worship and ornaments, as well as whatever smacks of wealth in their buildings and works, taking into account the social conditions of the people among whom they live."[6]

This poverty of the order, Father Karl Rahner says, is in our times a condition for the poverty of its members. "A really rich order or congregation can have no poor members, only members who are absolutely dependent on the community for their material needs."[7] The same concept is extended to all missionaries by Bishop Geise of Bogor, Indonesia. In poorer countries, he says, they must live poorly, build poor buildings, take on the poverty of the place. When people complain that his school will not last ten years, the bishop replies: "But it fits the environment, doesn't it?"[8]

For many at the Council, the survival of the Church seemed at stake. Bishop Joseph Blomjous of Tanzania, for example, was particularly concerned with the sociological projections if the Church failed to discard its Western dress in non-Western cultures. Between 1900 and 1940, a bright future was anticipated for the Church in what was then the colonial world of Asia and Africa, as well as in independent countries like China in a semicolonial relationship to the West. Statistics showed a rapid advance almost everywhere. The majority religions—Confucianism, Buddhism, Hinduism, and Animism—seemed to be sharing in the eclipse and decay of the cultures to which they were tied. The triumphant expanse of Western civilization

---

[5] Quoted in O'Grady, *op. cit.*, p. 35.

[6] *Acta Apostolicae Sedis,* 56 (1964), p. 568.

[7] "Die Armut des Ordenslebens in einer veränderten Welt," in *Geist und Leben,* 33 (1960), p. 265.

[8] Quoted in *America,* 113 (September 4, 1965), p. 228.

promised a quick absorption of all peoples into one world, the world of Christianity.

The collapse of colonialism after World War II has altered that picture fundamentally. A revival of indigenous cultures followed the withdrawal of the imperial powers. A new dynamism and even militancy of the old religions developed, as with Buddhism in southeast Asia, almost always with intensified pressures against Christianity.

Westerns were shocked by some of these developments. There was, of course, little surprise when China's Communists began to treat Christians as earlier Communists had treated them in Russia and Eastern Europe. It followed from their antireligious principles. It was logical for them to expel foreign missionaries and dragoon the local bishops and priests into cutting ties with Rome. But why did India, Ceylon, and Indonesia pursue a parallel policy of restricting the entry of foreign missionaries? Why did they and the new countries of Africa want to get control of the schools, hospitals, and other institutions with which these same missionaries had enriched their countries?

Such questions simply revealed the West's ignorance of the history of colonialism. In both Asia and Africa, Christian missionaries had often been the forerunners of the imperialists. They had been at work in Vietnam, for example, for some 250 years before the French occupied that region. The "duty" of protecting the properties and institutes of Christian missionaries often served as a pretext for imperialistic ventures. The missionaries themselves at times invited and encouraged the invaders and served as informants for them.

Where Europeans took over, the missionaries gave them and their children preferential treatment in schools and hospitals, and became in practice a part of the colonial machine. Not infrequently, they participated in the race policies and restrictive practices of the regime. One well-known secondary school functioned in East Africa for 75 years without ever admitting a single Negro. Even today it has only token integration several years after the country in which it operates has become independent under a Negro government.

Suspicion of the missionaries has, accordingly, a solid basis in history. It is reasonable for the newly independent governments to ask if the missions are not today a rear guard of the withdrawing imperialists, a possible fifth column left to prepare their return. In addition, the governments of countries whose economy permits health, welfare, and education services for only a minority of their people understandably consider themselves more entitled than some foreign interest to determine who should be given preference. The missionaries favor their fellow religionists, but is it proper to concentrate education and the resulting economic and political power in the hands of a religious minority? And is this even likely to benefit that minority in the long run? Will it not rather bring persecution on it as an obstacle to equal opportunity for other citizens?

Even before Vatican II, many churchmen in the new countries had been reading the signs and asking such questions. The Council gave them an opportunity for exchanges of views and reports on initiatives. The bishops of Tanzania, for example, did not wait for the government to seize their schools, as many others did. Instead, they went on record as recognizing the logic of government control and as ready to co-operate in an organized and constructive transfer of such control. They agreed that the time had come to withdraw from the institutions that had traditionally occupied much of the Church's activity in Western culture and that had served to introduce it to the non-Western world. As they saw it, the future social activity of the Church would have to be different.

But if different, what should it be? The question was easier to ask than to answer. As many saw it, a full answer is not yet possible. The modern missions from the West had been conducted on the no longer admissible principle that Western culture must be the vehicle for Christianity's expansion. Westerns would retain control of the so-called mission territories until they had formed an indigenous clerical elite thoroughly impregnated in their ways. The perpetuation of the entire religious-cultural package they had brought as God's gift and theirs to the "heathen" would thus be guaranteed.

The result was a series of distortions. The missionary inevitably regarded himself as superior, the guardian of values not understood by those to whom he was sent. He convinced himself that the new Christians could not for many generations be entrusted with major Church decisions. He decided that the way to train docile helpers was to withdraw children at an early age from their culture, raise them in schools allowing a minimum of contact with families and friends, instill in them a profound appreciation of the Western way of life and a corresponding repugnance for the traditional ways from which they had providentially been withdrawn. It took a very strong character to survive such an experience and reach manhood without a crippling inferiority complex. Those who did survive were ignorant of the traditions of their ancestors and consequently were ill-equipped to Christianize their people.

When Rome saw the political writing on the wall, it began a desperate scramble to reverse its course. But the crash program of de-Westernizing the Church in Asia and Africa had to be built on narrow foundations. As far as China was concerned, it was apparently too late. Elsewhere, the process continues at a different rhythm in each place. The new insights into the nature of the Church and of the liturgy provided by Vatican II have helped to clarify the fact that many countries hitherto ruled as spiritual colonies of the West are already well-established Churches, more solid than some that earlier in Western Europe lost the masses of the workers and have as yet made but a token return into the dechristianized layers of the population. The principle is consequently now well recognized that such Churches are not only entitled but obliged to assume responsibility for their own development, to determine the kinds of institutions they should have and the directions in which they should grow.

Application of this principle will not mean a withdrawal of Western missionaries. On the contrary, the principle of collegiality entitles the new Churches to demand a far bigger share of the personnel and other resources of the older Churches than they have been receiving. But the missionary's function will be similar to that of the technicians sent by the United Nations and by economically advanced countries to the developing nations of Asia and Africa. They will be advisers and administrators, not makers of policy.

Such redefinition of function has had a traumatic impact, not only on many missionaries as individuals but on the mission societies in Europe and the United States. They, in practice, thought of themselves, and were thought of by Rome and by the Churches from which they sprang, as being given the exclusive commission of preaching the Gospel in non-Christian lands. The Congregation for the Propagation of the Faith, a part of the Roman Curia, entrusted certain territories to each. In missionizing these territories, the institutional interests of the order or society often took precedence over other considerations. Even when a local Church was solidly established, its bishop was always a member of the mission society. Often the society excluded local candidates from membership, or accepted only a token number. Its control thus remained in the country of its origin or in Rome. If vocations flourished in the diocese, the local priests had a second-class status. The most thriving and wealthy parishes, for example, were reserved for priests of the mission society.

Much of the discussion at the Council of the decree on the Church's missionary activity reflected the search for solutions to such problems. The decree did not analyze them specifically, but its approach was designed to deal with them. The first work of the missionary, it said, is to establish dialogue with non-Christians, leading to conversion, teaching of the truths of faith, and training in the Christian way of life. After this Christian initiation comes the Baptism that forms a Christian community with deep roots in the culture of the country itself. Once such a Christian community has come into being, its most urgent task is to train a local clergy, including a local bishop who now becomes the center for unity in his diocese and determines its organization. The Council decree recognized that new arrangements must be made to govern relations between such bishops and the missionary institutes. Rather than attempt to draft universally applicable rules, it wisely assigned the task to national and regional conferences of bishops.

The change in status and authority is not going to be easy for the mission institutes. Vatican II has nevertheless shown that change is theologically demanded, just as it was already clear that it has become politically essential. This does not, however, mean that the need for help from the mission institutes will become less necessary. Only about a quarter of the priests in Africa are Africans. Although the number of African priests doubled between 1949 and 1963, there was a parallel increase in the number of Catholics.

In another sphere, the decree on the adaptation and renewal of the religious orders rejected the legalistic interpretations of poverty as merely obligating the members to have their superior's approval for what they use. They must, it says, be poor "both in fact and in spirit." The religious community as a whole must, in addition, "offer a quasi-collective witness to poverty," avoiding every appearance "of luxury, excessive wealth and the accumulation of goods."

New rules for the dress of monks and nuns similarly stressed the Council's desire that those pledged to poverty should appear poor. The dress must be changed, the decree says, if it is not "simple and modest, poor and at the same time becoming, meeting the requirements of health, and suited to the circumstances of time and place and to the needs of the ministry involved." If intelligently implemented, this instruction will remove a small but important obstacle to dialogue between the Church and the world, and also between laity and clergy within the Church.

A few general directives on the meaning of the vow of poverty of monks and nuns may seem a very tiny mouse to emerge from the mountainous discussions of poverty within the Council itself and the less formal exchanges among the Fathers during the Council. Implementing their letter and spirit, nevertheless, will entail a profound change of mentality in many convents and monasteries. These organizations, with their schools, colleges, hospitals, and other institutions, play a major part in creating the community image of the Church in all countries, but especially in the underdeveloped world in which they form the spearhead of the missions. If they can come to understand that their walled enclaves and expensive garb not only cut the poor off from them but also cut them off from the poor, the effect could be catalytic.

Apart from the recommendations for monks and nuns, the concrete results of Vatican II in regard to poverty are not overwhelming. Some small simplifications were introduced into papal ceremonial. A considerable number of bishops began to wear a wooden cross. At the closing ceremony of the Council, Pope Paul gave each bishop a plain gold-plated ring as a souvenir, and the hope was expressed unofficially that the bishops would sell their jeweled ring and use the proceeds for charity.

Already during the Council, Pope Paul had used his history-making visits outside Italy to dramatize the Church's concern for the world's poor. He let it be known that the idea of going to the Holy Land had first occurred to him while reading Father Paul Gauthier's *The Poor, Jesus and the Church*. In India, at the Eucharistic Congress in Bombay, he appealed to all countries to contribute large parts of the resources they were spending on arms to a world-wide effort to combat poverty, to provide food, clothing, and decent housing for the millions who lack them. That appeal he recalled and repeated at the United Nations in October 1965. And, praising the work of the UN and its associated bodies for the ignorant, the diseased, and the poor of the world, he asserted that the only way to build peace was to eliminate hunger from the world.

The Council statement on the Church in the Modern World included several comments on poverty. Everyone, it said, has a right to a share of earthly goods sufficient for himself and his family; and if one is in extreme necessity, he is entitled to take what he needs from the riches of others. But if men lived up to their obligations, the Council added, such a situation would not even arise. "Man should regard the external things that he legitimately possesses not only as his own but also as common in the sense that they should be able to benefit not only him but also others."

The duty to help, the Council stressed, is not simply to feed the hungry but to create conditions in which "they may be able to help and develop themselves." It extends not only to one's own community or country but to the entire world. "Those Christians are to be praised and supported who volunteer their services to help other men and nations. Indeed, it is the duty of the whole people of God, following the word and example of the bishops, to alleviate as far as they are able the sufferings of the modern age. They should do this too, as was the ancient custom of the Church, out of the substance of their goods and not only out of what is superfluous."

While praising aid from the rich nations to the poor, the Council was extremely critical of some of the abuses that have characterized aid in the period since World War II. Foreign specialists, it said, should "not act as overlords, but as helpers and fellow workers." Help should be given "with generosity and without greed on the one side, and received with complete honesty on the other." To establish a genuine world economic order, "an end will have to be put to profiteering, to national ambitions, to the appetite for political supremacy, to militaristic calculations, and to machinations for the sake of spreading and imposing ideologies." Here, said the Council, is a challenge to the sincerity of all Christians. "Do not let men, then, be scandalized because some countries with a majority of citizens who are counted as Christians have an abundance of wealth, whereas others are deprived of the necessities of life and are tormented with hunger, disease, and every kind of misery. The spirit of poverty and charity are the glory and witness of the Church of Christ."

As its final word on the subject of poverty, the Council decided to add, at the very end of the statement on the Church in the Modern World, a recommendation for a permanent secretariat. "Considering the immensity of the hardships which still afflict the greater part of mankind today," it said, "the Council regards it as most opportune that an organism of the universal Church be set up in order that both the justice and love of Christ toward the poor might be developed everywhere. The role of such an organism would be to stimulate the Catholic community to promote progress in needy regions and international social justice."

When the new secretariat goes into operation, it will undoubtedly establish just how deep the impact of the Council's meditation on poverty has been on the life of the Church. One was left at the end of the Council with the impression that many conflicting views on this subject could still be found at the highest levels of the Church's leadership. Some would happily develop the proposed secretariat into a super-ministry to co-ordinate and strengthen the Vatican's economic and financial structures. The result could be an impressive contribution to current national and international efforts to aid in world development. But it could also strengthen the already widespread image of the Church as an integral part and perhaps a tool of the wealthy classes and the wealthy nations. Others would have a secretariat whose main task would be to create a world understanding of the rights of the poor and to urge Christians to lead in implementing those rights. This latter course would fit in better with the ecumenical approach to mission work. It would also be more consonant with the sense of the Council that one of the Church's urgent tasks is to renew itself in poverty.

Chapter 7

The Church Seeks a Partnership

For a thousand years, from Constantine to the Late Renaissance, the Church was at the center of civilized life. Church and state were considered perfect societies, each in its own sphere, but the Church was the higher of the two because of its more exalted function. Churchmen claimed—and to a large extent were accorded—primary authority over broad areas of overlapping jurisdiction, that is, the realm of ideas, of education, of culture.

This framework provided a satisfactory working hypothesis for the Middle Ages. The great secular cultures of Greece and Rome had been pulverized by the onslaughts of the barbarians. The Church was sole custodian of both spiritual and religious values. And it tended them so well as to create once more a dynamic civil society, conscious of its rights and its needs. Gradually, however, educated men began to see that the material progress of which Western Europe was capable called for an independent development of the arts and sciences. Such development required an atmosphere of freedom from the restraints that churchmen imposed when they subordinated worldly concerns to those of the other life as they conceived it.

The Church's failure to recognize the forces it had set in motion produced the breach between the Church and the world that we have inherited. For four centuries, mankind's great hopes have been borne by scientists and thinkers who were usually not professing Christians and who were often in violent conflict with a Church they saw as a brake on human progress. The gulf was widened to a distance long regarded as unbridgeable when the theory of evolution was formulated in the nineteenth century. The immediate reaction of the Church's spokesmen was to reject this interpretation of creation as a direct contradiction of truths contained in the Scriptures. As evidence in its support mounted, they made grudging concessions. For *The Catholic Encyclopedia,* published in New York in 1909 and reprinted without change until 1960, evolution was still an unproved hypothesis. There was "no evidence in favor of an ascending evolution of organic forms . . . no trace of even a merely probable argument in favor of the animal origin of man."

Such an attitude on the part of believers forced modern man to lead his life independently of the Church and to regard himself as emotionally in hopeless conflict with it. Those Catholics who recognized that the polemic was not necessary had difficulty in making their voices heard. Even when historical and scientific evidence had accumulated to establish evolution as not merely a theory but a fact, an atmosphere of obscurantism slowed down the circulation and acceptance of evolution among Catholics. Many who intellectually accepted the truth of evolution retained their emotional resistance. They failed to put this truth to work for themselves and for mankind.

The one who did most to change this attitude within the Church was the French Jesuit Teilhard de Chardin. His working hypothesis, evolved between the First and Second World Wars, offers a new concept of the notion of creation. In the traditional Catholic view, God had made the world in a single act, giving to each thing its nature and functions, with man as the highest pinnacle of material creation, lord of everything else, but himself subject to a series of rules established by God. Man's time on earth was reduced to "a period of testing," an interval with no intrinsic values of its own. When it ended, he would be rewarded if he had observed the rules, punished if he had violated them.

Such an interpretation of life was acceptable in a primitive society in which man's control of his environment was marginal. It served to rationalize the apparent meaninglessness of the existence of the masses whose lives lacked material comfort and intellectual development. Because of such long-standing assumptions, St. Thomas Aquinas was able to follow Aristotle in defending slavery as consonant with man's dignity. But the expansion of the area of man's control over the world and the discovery and harnessing of forces capable of giving the good life to all men finally made the interpretation superfluous. The concurrent development of a deeper appreciation of man as a rational being with inherent dignity and rights made it offensive.

Teilhard de Chardin offered a more dynamic view. As he saw it, creation belongs at the end of world history rather than at the beginning. The last stroke of the brush completes the artist's work. The last act of history will be the completion of God's creative work. The progress from the beginning of the world to this point still comes from God through the forces and powers accorded to things at the start of the creative process. The difference is that man is no longer presented as playing in God's garden, still less as a plaything of God to be rewarded or punished according to his skill in performing a series of moral exercises. He is an associate of God in the creative process. Every act of development of the world, whether performed by believer or nonbeliever, thus becomes a creative act. Every obstruction of the political, social, economic, or cultural progress of the world is a holding back of creation. Christ is here seen as not only the Redeemer of man in the traditional Christian sense, but also as the one holding the central place in the continuing creative process, so that He has primacy over every creature.

Viewed in this perspective, the world in which we live partakes of an implicit Christianity—not on the supernatural level, as in the life of the baptized Christian renewed by grace, but as a sanctified expression of man's communion with God. The Christian, accordingly, should not see a conflict or even a contrast between two dimensions of his life, the sacred and the profane. Instead, he is offered two complementary, authentically Christian expressions of one and the same God-related life concealed in the mystery of Christ.

Is is not known how directly Pope John was influenced by Teilhard. But Monsignor Pietro Pavan, who was close to John at the Vatican, was an immense admirer of Teilhard and did not hesitate to speak favorably about him to a conference of

Catholic university students shortly after the Holy Office in 1962 warned the rectors of seminaries and universities to protect their students "against the dangers contained in his works." And John himself discussed the importance of Teilhard's work when he received Poet-President L. Sedar Senghor of Senegal in audience.

Accordingly, it is not surprising to find that Pope John shared Teilhard's positive attitude to the world, his awareness of the great reservoirs of goodness waiting to be tapped. He saw the world as already in Christ, so that the task of the Church was to make the world understand that fact. The Fathers echoed that belief in the message they addressed to the world early in the Council's first session. They hoped, they said, "to announce to the men of our age God's truth in its fullness and purity in such a way that it will be understood and fully accepted by them."

The ideas expressed in this statement quickly crystallized into a project for a formal document to express the Church's reawakened desire for dialogue with the world. At the end of the first session, Cardinal Suenens of Belgium proposed that the Council's entire program should be concentrated on two aspects of the Church, first its own nature and mission, and second its relation to the world. The decree on the nature of the Church would thus be complemented by another great document as its opposite pole. This would force the Church in the Council not to be concerned with itself alone, with its own structures and officials. It would always have to be conscious that its reason for existence was to bring salvation to the world.

The idea won ready approval. At the level of principle, there was no conflict between progressives and conservatives, traditionalists or innovators. Implementation, however, was something else. No sooner were the first attempts made to formulate the Church's views about the contemporary world than it became necessary to face up to two facts: a progressive estrangement of Church and world had occurred over the last few hundred years; and the blame for that estrangement rested on the Church as well as on the world.

A new evaluation of some of the most cherished attitudes of churchmen was thus demanded. The world had developed its own positions on the relations of church and state, on the right of every man to follow his conscience in his beliefs and in their expression, on the need for freedom from external restraint in the search for truth, on the concept of obedience to authority, on the place and function of the mass media in society. Many conservative churchmen were convinced that the common contemporary attitudes were incompatible with the Christian faith. Others found themselves so dependent on their own institutionalized situation that they could not conceive of an adjustment as radical as that demanded by the world. Some thought that withdrawal of state aid would bankrupt Catholic institutions and leave the clergy destitute. Others felt that opening up traditionally Catholic countries to Protestant missionaries would lead to a massive loss of faith.

Even in a country like the United States, in which the Church was independent of state subsidies, many confused the questioning of the traditional methods of exercising authority with a challenge to the principle of authority in the Church. Others were reluctant to face the necessary transformation of the Catholic press from a series of house organs at the service of the institutionalized Church, dedicated to projecting the views of the hierarchy to the mass of the faithful, into organs of public opinion within the Church, reflecting and expressing the views of the entire people of God.

Others, while willing to face the issues honestly, were not always sure that the Council was equipped to give worth-while answers to many concrete issues affecting the world's peace, prosperity, and freedom, even its continued existence. Could a commission of bishops and theologians assemble the needed expert knowledge to say anything valuable or even valid about the population explosion, nuclear warfare, disarmament, or the development of the new nations? In the light of the obvious lack of agreement among the Fathers on many such vital issues, would not a statement confined to the narrow areas of agreement perhaps be more harmful than beneficial to the desired dialogue of Church and world?

Notwithstanding such arguments, the Council recognized that it neither could nor should operate in an ivory tower. Everything it did necessarily involved conclusions in the practical order. The restoration of the faithful to active participation in the Church's life, set in motion by the decrees on the liturgy and on the nature of the Church, inescapably raised the issue of public opinion in the Church. The statement on relations between Jews and Christians compelled a dialogue not only with Jews but with many others outside the visible Church who considered themselves affected. The Council saw that it had no alternative but to start a re-evaluation of the Church's relations with the world.

One vital area concerned the Church's understanding and use of the means by which knowledge is circulated among men, the press and other media of mass communications. This was, from the outset, a practical concern for the Council. It needed to inform both Catholics and the many interested and sympathetic outsiders.

Mass communications developed at a time of extreme estrangement of Church and world in the eighteenth and nineteenth centuries. Open hostility marked relations of the Vatican with most of the Italian press even into the twentieth century. Vatican officials, frequently underpaid, made a practice of selling information to friendly newspapers. The result was a kind of managed news, but managed in the interests of those involved more than in the interests of the Church or of truth.

The secrecy imposed at the First Vatican Council did not keep the issues or the passions out of the newspapers. Instead, it multiplied misinformation and unfounded fears. Abbot Butler, English historian of the Council, blamed secrecy for the climate of diffidence and suspicions. This gave a free hand and a clear field to the hostile press, while the bishops—bound to secrecy—could not deal effectively with rumors.[1]

Vatican thinking on the press changed little between 1870 and 1962. The Second Vatican Council opened with the same commitment to secrecy as the First and the same concept of managed leakage of news to selected publications. Through their curial connections, some Roman newspapers gave almost verbatim reports of what some bishops said at the daily meetings, the accounts being consistently slanted to favor the curial viewpoints. Meanwhile, the Council press office reports were superficial, confused, concerned largely with external trivia, and slanted.

[1] See E. E. Y. Hales, *The Catholic Church in the Modern World* (New York, Doubleday Image Books, 1960), p. 140.

The French and German bishops quickly saw that the Council could founder on this rock. Bypassing the official press office, they arranged full coverage for Catholic publications in their two countries. The first significant help for the English-language press was given by American-born Father Ralph Wiltgen. During the first session he arranged 18 press conferences at which Council Fathers and theology experts explained issues under discussion. Xavier Rynne and Robert Kaiser developed their own information sources to present, in *The New Yorker* and *Time* respectively, analyses in depth of the great soul-searching the bishops had begun in St. Peter's. Many shocked ecclesiastics protested that these reports were unjustifiably sensational, but their substantial accuracy was finally confirmed. The alert enterprise of these two reporters and the competence of their magazine articles and of the books they later published played a major role in enabling the world to understand the meaning of the Council.

Bowing to the universal demand for more news, Archbishop Felici, the Council's secretary general, announced at the start of the second session in September 1963 that the press would get a better break. The meetings would no longer be secret. However, they still remained closed to the press, and the discussions might be divulged only with "the greatest prudence and moderation."

What this meant to the official press office was indicated by its first communiqué under the new system. It listed the names of the speakers and summarized their comments on a document, the name or nature of which was nowhere described in the release. Nor was it possible to determine which speaker expressed what view.

Father Edward Heston, C.S.C., fortunately had a different idea of what "the greatest prudence and moderation" required. He had been assigned to brief the English-language press, and he did so with the precision and fullness the reporters wanted. The United States bishops had, in addition, assembled a group of theologians, canonists, liturgists, historians, and other specialists. Like Father Heston, they attended the meetings and had access to the documents. They met the press for an hour each afternoon, answering questions and supplementing the information earlier supplied by Father Heston from their own observation and interpretation.

Those assigned to brief the French, Germans, and others quickly followed Father Heston's lead. The Council press office tried to restrain them, but the bishops to whom they were answerable realized that nothing less than honest reporting would satisfy the press and serve the Council. The official press office finally bowed to the inevitable and began to produce factual communiqués. It was a big step forward. To project the proceedings in terms of medieval pomp and splendor, as the Curia had wished, would have thwarted Pope John's aim of making the Church meaningful to the world. Fortunately for the Church, the press was too powerful, too intelligent, and too sympathetic to co-operate in that error.

The compromise for which the press settled was, nevertheless, far from ideal. Enough "news" was provided to keep the daily newspapers and the wire services happy. But the segment of the proceedings singled out for semiexposure, the daily general meeting, was arbitrary. Father Heston and his colleagues did a splendid job of selection. But a rapid 50-word summary of 1,500 words in a closely reasoned Latin text could not always extract its full flavor. If the headlines were sometimes misleading, one could blame the Council's refusal to release texts to those asked to report their nuances.

The U.S. bishops' panel of experts, while of considerable help, was also handicapped by its terms of reference. Its members might explain only what had been said on the floor. When there was a maneuver to thwart the will of the majority, they could not comment or reveal knowledge they possessed.

Another defect was that a written intervention submitted by a Council Father to save time or because debate was cut off before his name was reached, was concealed from the press. Archbishop Roberts, an outspoken critic of the Holy Office, said in late 1965 that not one of his many requests to speak had been honored, not even when he had handed in his name several months before the particular item was to be discussed.

It is true that a council Father was free to hand out the text of his talk or of his written intervention to anyone he chose. But the rank-and-file newsman was here at a serious disadvantage as against those who had inside contacts or were working for influential newspapers. The rank-and-file bishop was equally at a disadvantage as against his wealthy or well-placed colleagues who could achieve wide diffusion of their viewpoints among newsmen. When that was combined with the Council's failure to develop machinery to determine how far a given viewpoint had substantial backing or reflected a lone holdout, one can see that the best-intentioned newsman could easily become the innocent tool of minority interests. Six speeches on one side and three on the other looked like a two-to-one sweep. Actually, the three might be talking for two thousand, the six for sixty.

Another inequity was one with a long Roman history. Not all newsmen were excluded from the Council meetings. Many got in as theological experts, as secretaries to bishops, as observers, auditors, or "special guests" of someone with access to passes. They could get copies of restricted documents, visit the coffee bars in St. Peter's where decisions were reached and news made. They had an unfair advantage over their colleagues.

The denial to the press of facilities it would be accorded at any other international conference flowed in part from an absence of technical competence. Church structures tend to lag behind the times, and this is eminently true of its central structures. Officials trained in the ecclesiastical sciences are placed in posts requiring an entirely different kind of education and experience. Even when technicians are available to advise them, they are reluctant to listen.

There was, however, a deeper reason for the Council's failure to utilize the media of communications effectively. As indicated above, Vatican officialdom suffers from a basic misconception of the function of the press. For example, Archbishop Felici, the Council general secretary, said in November 1964 that newsmen covering the Council were "parasites and fungi . . . promoting confusion, insubordination and error." Alluding to Scripture for support, he compared them to the cockle in the wheat, to be tolerated until the end of the Council as "a necessary evil."[2]

Here we are back a century or more to that aristocratic bias of Catholic theologians and historians who, following the

[2] *L'Osservatore Romano* (November 29, 1964).

French Revolution, identified the masses with the mobs and blamed the popular press for inciting the mobs to violence against civil and religious authority. This is the mentality that considers the mass newspaper to be intrinsically evil, a scandal sheet, an arbitrary power structure, to be manipulated by trickery equal to its own, capable of being bought, and itself ready to buy what will serve its ends.

That misunderstanding of the press was not confined to strictly curial circles was shown by the Council's decree on the press, radio, cinema, and television. A draft prepared by a committee distinguished mostly by its lack of professional qualifications for its task was introduced at the first session. It was full of pious condemnations of perversions of the information media and of exhortations to develop wholesome and instructive publications, films, and so on. It attributed to the press a teaching function foreign to its nature. It laid down principles that would favor not only ecclesiastical but civil censorship of the press and other media, principles that would, in fact, equally justify Communist states in the restrictions they impose on religious publications.

The Council discussed the draft decree on communications briefly and superficially in November 1962, approved it in principle, and told the drafting committee to shorten it. The decree came back a year later with fewer words but with most of its former defects. Some indication of its contents had by now filtered through the curtain of secrecy, bringing anguished protests from professional newsmen. A few of the Fathers attempted a last-minute action. They first asked the Council's executive committee to postpone voting to allow a re-evaluation by experts. When this was refused, 25 Fathers of 20 different nationalities signed a brief note for distribution to their colleagues. It urged rejection of the document as failing to measure up to the expectations of Christians, particularly of specialists, and as calculated to harm the Council's prestige. Simultaneously, a group of leading Catholic newsmen published a criticism of some of the document's more glaring defects.

Arrangements were made to distribute the note signed by the 25 Fathers outside St. Peter's, as had been done with two notes calling for a negative vote on issues to which the conservative minority was opposed. This time, however, papal guards were sent to stop the distribution. Cardinal Tisserant, senior member of the Curia, protested at the opening of the session against improper attempts to influence the vote, and Archbishop Felici said that a Father whose name was on the note had told him he had not signed it. When the vote was counted, the negatives were still nearly one out of four, but not enough to prevent passage. Later, many Fathers admitted that they had never read the text.

In some other areas, however, the Council was more successful in bringing its thinking into step with that of the contemporary world. A good example is religious freedom. The non-Christian world and many Christians consider the Catholic Church intolerant and totalitarian in its teaching and practice on the right of others to live and express their religious beliefs. They base their position not only on such historical evidence as that provided by the Inquisition and the condemnation of Galileo. In this century also, they say, Catholics have continued to approve restraints on the rights of members of other faiths in Spain and Colombia. Catholic pressure groups in the United States have sought to introduce or retain laws on censorship and contraception reflecting their own moral code but not that of the general community. Even though the non-Christian often considers sixteenth-century Protestants as more intolerant than Catholics, he points out that subsequent Protestant history was more influenced by the stress of the post-Christian philosophers on the dignity of man and the inalienable rights of his conscience.

The analysis is substantially true. Until very recently, most Catholic theologians insisted that the Church should enjoy religious freedom where it was a minority, but where the Church was a majority they denied equal treatment to others. It was the famous distinction of thesis and hypothesis. For them the thesis, or normal situation, was intolerance in a Catholic state. The hypothesis, or special situation, was tolerance where non-Catholics were so numerous that they could not be pushed around.

Catholic theologians in the United States were among the first to challenge this view. The older position was that the state had an obligation to support the Catholic Church and discriminate against other religions. The experience of the Church in the United States under a regime of separation of Church and state made American Catholic theologians begin a re-evaluation. It led them to the conclusion that friendly separation was not only better for the Church in practice but was a more logical theory.

Catholic theologians elsewhere long resisted the American view, some denouncing it as close to heresy. However, the expansion of Communism after World War II produced second thoughts. In Eastern Europe the Communists were delighted to take over the previous system and use it for their own ends. Their constitutions proclaimed separation of the state *from* the Church, a subtle but important variation on the American expression of separation of Church and state. Their practice, however, became and remains one of dictation by the state to the Churches, using the very same arguments by which Catholic theologians had sought to make the state the executive arm of the Church in the pursuit of its objectives.

In Latin America, the Mexican Revolution destroyed a Catholic Church institutionalized in the forms prescribed by the "thesis" and introduced complete separation. In the historic circumstances, the emotional climate was a hostile one. Within a quarter of a century, nevertheless, the Church in Mexico developed an internal dynamism comparable to that of the United States, leaving far behind the other Latin American countries which either enjoyed or dreamed of regaining a position of privilege in society.

Pope John went on record in *Pacem in terris* as favoring full freedom of conscience for everyone, and he approved of the idea that the Council should similarly express itself in favor of religious freedom. All was not clear sailing, however. Cardinal Bea and Cardinal Ottaviani came up with two very different drafts. A mixed commission named by Pope John to unify the two never met. Finally, the task was given to Cardinal Bea's Secretariat for Christian Unity, subject to approval of the revision by Cardinal Ottaviani's Theological Commission.

Ottaviani was not alone in his opposition. In addition to the important intrinsic issues, the statement raised the problem of repudiating what was for a considerable time the official teaching of Rome as expressed by various popes. When, after much maneuvering, debate was opened in November 1963, the persistence of the old view became evident. To the great disappointment of many, particularly of the bishops of the United States, debate was adjourned without any vote having been taken. It was freely prophesied that no more would be heard of the project.

The gloom was premature. In September 1964, a text profoundly modified in the light of 380 written comments submitted by Fathers came up for further discussion. By now it had become clear that a large majority favored a declaration, but that within this majority wide divergences existed. A French-led group wanted a statement based strictly on the Scriptures. It would be a prophetic text presenting God's mysterious respect for the freedom with which He has endowed man and which He expands by His grace. Another group, which was strongly supported by bishops from the United States and whose spokesman was Father John Courtney Murray, wanted a document that would start from the dignity of the human being as such and develop man's right to freedom in religious matters vis-à-vis civil society and the state, along lines parallel to those of the Charter of the United Nations and its Declaration of Human Rights. A third position sought to reaffirm primarily the freedom of the Church, that is to say, the rights of the true religion, particularly in relation to Communist interference with those rights.

The third position was the easiest to dispose of. Time and again, a move was started to have the Council condemn Communism, but each time it was beaten off. It has been plausibly suggested that an understanding existed between Rome and Moscow guaranteeing that in return for the visas granted to many bishops from East Europe and to the Orthodox observers from behind the Iron Curtain the Council would refrain from attacks on the Communist system. What is certain is that Pope John showed that he did not believe a repetition of the clear condemnations already on the record would serve any constructive purpose, and the Council majority consistently backed that view.

The differences between the French and the American positions were harder to resolve. There was some yielding on both sides, but the final version reflects principally the American ap-

proach. Two arguments proved particularly telling. One was
that the biblical bases were far from convincing, that one could
say the proposed declaration was in conformity with the Scriptures, and particularly with Christ's words and acts, but that
clear scriptural proofs were lacking. The second was that what
the world would understand and appreciate would be a statement based on the nature of man as such.

It would follow from the logic of the document that the state
should maintain absolute neutrality as between different religions. A substantial minority of the Fathers, nevertheless,
could not stomach so radical a departure from a firm position of
every pope from Gregory XVI to Pius XII, all of whom had
worked assiduously to obtain privileges for the Church from
any government that could be persuaded to grant them. To
appease this minority, a formula was developed that in fact
meant a reversal of the earlier thesis-hypothesis. Even if the
peculiar circumstances of a particular country cause one religious community to receive special civil recognition, it said,
the right of other religious communities and of all citizens to
religious freedom should be acknowledged and made effective.
By this clause, the Council recognized that in special circumstances a state might have an established religion, provided that the rights of other religions were not restricted; but
henceforth for Catholics separation of Church and state would
be normal.

Returning to the subject of church-state relations in the
statement on the Church in the Modern World, the Council reaffirmed its preference for friendly separation of the powers.
The Church and the political community in their own field, it
said, "are autonomous and independent from each other." While
making use of temporal things insofar as its own mission requires, the Church does not place its trust "in the privileges
offered by civil authority. The Church will even give up the
exercise of certain rights that have been legitimately acquired if
it becomes clear that their use will cast doubt on the sincerity
of the Church's witness or that new ways of life demand new
methods." The Church asks only "true freedom to preach the
faith, to teach its social doctrine, to exercise its role freely
among men, and also to pass moral judgment in those matters

which regard public order when the fundamental rights of a person or the salvation of souls require it."

These comments on religious freedom may be taken as typical of what the Fathers tried to do in the whole statement on the Church and the Modern World. It is an effort to show that the Church has views—positive, progressive views—on everything that is of practical concern to contemporary mankind, while avoiding the temptation to give ready-made answers to complicated problems. It is a document that will not fully satisfy anyone, but this follows from its very nature.

The specific purpose of the document is itself interesting. The answer is presented early in the text: "Under the light of Christ . . . the Council wishes to speak to all men in order to shed light on the mystery of man and to co-operate in finding the solution to the outstanding problems of our time." It is not an attempt to tell the world how it should behave, but simply to explain how Christians view the purpose of their lives, so that others can know what to expect of them, and in what areas and under what conditions they can co-operate for community purposes.

The document begins, accordingly, by pointing out that the commitment of the Christian to the present life is not total. He believes he has a higher destiny, one so much more important than his transitory life on earth that all his judgments must be made in relation to it. In a Teilhardian perspective, however, it insists that his faith does not lessen the Christian's commitment to man's progress on earth, because his final destiny can be achieved only by due concern for earthly activities. "The Church sincerely professes that all men, believers and unbelievers alike, ought to work for the rightful betterment of this world in which all alike live." Human activity directed to the improvement of living conditions "accords with God's will. For man, created to God's image, received a mandate to subject to himself the earth and all it contains. . . . This mandate concerns the whole of everyday activity. . . . The triumphs of the human race are a sign of God's grace and a flowering of His mysterious design."

Having created this basis for collaboration, the Council went on to describe the part that the Church itself could play in helping the world to reach its own proper goals of human development. Abandoning the cherished claim to be the sole light and guide for mankind in a sea of darkness, the Council presented the Church as made up of sinful men who have in many circumstances historically allied themselves with reactionary forces and institutions that held back the proper progress of mankind. Such mistakes, however, did not flow from the nature of the Church's mission but resulted from a misunderstanding of it because of "the human failings of those to whom the Gospel is entrusted."

Having thus made clear that the Church could not only help but also be helped by the world, the Council took a further significant step. Even for its own members, it said, the Church does not always have answers, not even on urgent moral issues. "The Church guards the heritage of God's word and draws moral and religious principles without always having at hand solutions to particular problems." What it can do and seeks to do is to add the light of revealed truth to mankind's store of experience, thereby increasing the enlightenment of its members in their duties and activities in the world. But this is the practical limit of its competence. The Council rejected the claim frequently made by churchmen that the Church was entitled to give the Catholic specific guidance in his activities as a citizen. "Laymen should also know that it is generally the function of the well-informed Christian conscience to see that the divine law is inscribed in the life of the earthly city; from priests they may look for spiritual light and nourishment. Let the layman not imagine that his pastors are always such experts that to every problem which arises, however complicated, they can readily give him a concrete solution, or even that such is their mission."

The point might have been made more logically in a document addressed directly to the members of the Church. Nevertheless, it is not out of place where it is. Others should understand the rejection by the Council of the pre-Johannine concept of the Church as a monolithic controller of thought and dictator of action for all its members in all areas of their lives. It is also a necessary clarification if the Council's recognition, later in the same document, of an inability to give concrete decisions on burning issues from birth control to nuclear warfare is to make sense.

The area in which the document speaks with most precision and sureness is that of the Church's attitude to socioeconomic development, a theme well developed in papal encyclicals from Leo XIII to John XXIII. Starting from the generally agreed principle that man's control of nature is now such as to enable him to satisfy the ever increasing needs of the human family, and that such satisfaction of needs is a proper object of human activity, it offers some guidelines for the task.

Justice, it says, demands the giving of top priority to ending the current monstrous economic inequalities both within nations and between rich and poor nations. The fundamental law of economic progress should not be the search for profit or power but the service of men without distinction of race or geographic location. Even though private property has its roots in the person and is closely related to human liberty, it must be subordinated to this higher aim. Private property can have various forms, and it should not be presented as an obstacle to public ownership demanded by the common good. A specific abuse of private property is the existence of huge estates in backward countries in which rural masses are landless and starving. Subject to this overriding need, however, the human values of distribution of ownership and of economic control are stressed. The document looks forward to a world in which the average man everywhere will live at a human level of comfort, in which men and nations will have a democratic share in the orientation of an economy dominated neither by individuals nor by the state, and in which organized labor will be represented in the management of industry.

On more specific issues, the document presents viewpoints that were in great part endorsed by Pope Paul on various occasions while it was still being discussed by the Council, and notably in his speech to the United Nations in October 1965. His "moral and solemn ratification" of the UN as "the necessary road of modern civilization and of world peace" parallels the document's insistence on the value of international organizations and the duty of the Christian to support and advance them. His call to the UN to develop its structures to their logical conclusions and to outlaw war as an instrument of national policy is an echo of the document's condemnation of "total war" and its support for a supranational authority with power to punish those who disturb the international order.

Here again, both pope and Council recognized their inability to resolve the issues that stand in the way of attaining the goals they propose. The "balance of terror" is a fact, a monstrous fact, but still a fact. The Council refused to condemn outright those who seek to maintain this balance by the manufacture and possession of weapons intended solely to discourage a potential aggressor. But it showed more clearly than the Church has ever done before, at least since the first centuries of its existence, that war is not the proper business of a Christian. Some American bishops did not like this position. It seemed to them a criticism of the current defense policies of the United States. Spokesmen for the majority insisted that they were concerned with principles and were not judging specific situations. But they beat down a last-minute effort led by Archbishop Philip Hannan of New Orleans to have the Fathers reject the statement.

Instead of a theology of war, accordingly, the Council made a start on a theology of peace. It praised those "who renounce the use of violence in the vindication of their rights and who resort to measures of defense that are otherwise available to weaker parties too." It took cognizance of the growing number of Christians and non-Christians who, as individuals, have made the further step of deciding that any participation in war is immoral. Legislation should be enacted everywhere, it said, to protect conscientious objectors. While the proposal created no problem for bishops from the United States or Britain, where the principle has long been recognized and rather fully implemented, it met strong opposition from many in Europe, especially bishops from France and Italy. The traditional association of the institutional Church and the state in Europe has created a climate in which the idea that an individual has the right to challenge "authority" is shocking.

While admitting a nation's right to defend itself and recognizing the legitimacy of military service, the Council was forthright in its condemnation of total war. "Any act of war aimed indiscriminately at the destruction of entire cities or extensive areas along with their population is a crime against God and man himself. It merits unequivocal and unhesitating condemnation." The arms race received a similar judgment: It is "an utterly treacherous trap for humanity, and one which ensnares the poor to an intolerable degree. It is much to be feared that if this race persists, it will eventually spawn all the lethal ruin whose path it is now making ready."

Every effort must be made to have war completely outlawed by international consent, a goal requiring "the establishment of some universal public authority acknowledged as such by all and endowed with the power to safeguard, on behalf of all, security, regard for justice, and respect for rights." The program envisaged would call for the progressive and parallel reduction of national arms, and then for their elimination when international structures gave promise of adequate protection.

The new emphasis on personal responsibility also emerges in a paragraph which stresses that a soldier cannot give blind obedience to the commands of his superior. Some Fathers questioned the wisdom of this declaration. While recognizing that this was the underlying principle in the war-guilt trials after World War II, they insisted that no state would allow a soldier to question the orders given him in wartime. The Council, nevertheless, felt that the principle deserved affirmation, even if states were unwilling to implement it. Man's conscience, it said, gives voice to the principles of universal natural law, and actions that conflict with them, as well as orders commanding such actions, are criminal. "Blind obedience cannot excuse those who yield to them. . . . The courage of those who fearlessly and openly resist those who issue such commands merits supreme commendation."

The extent to which the individual, including the individual Christian, must make his own decisions in the framework of his own existential situation was again stressed in the section devoted to marriage and the family. Marriage, mirroring the love that binds Christ and the Church, is presented in the perspective of personal love and fidelity, and children are envisaged as part of this community of persons. This represents a real advance over the former practice of presenting procreation as the primary aim of marriage and the growth in love of the parents as a secondary aim. The two aims are regarded as mutually related to each other, so that they are not placed in a hierarchical order.

This reformulation of the theology of marriage was bitterly but unsucessfully fought by the conservative theologians. They feared that the way was being opened for a change in the Church's teaching on contraception. To have agreed that the primary purpose of the sexual act is reproduction would have strengthened their assertion that no other purpose can justify the act when the primary purpose is excluded by artificial means.

The Council avoided such biological criteria in favor of human and personal criteria of morality. It stated that marriage was not instituted solely for procreation, that the sexual characteristics of man notably exceed those of lower forms of life, so that the acts proper to conjugal life, when exercised in accordance with genuine human dignity, are worthy of honor. It also recognized that abstinence is not a satisfactory method of family limitation. "Where the intimacy of married life is broken off, its faithfulness can sometimes be imperiled and its quality of fruitfulness ruined."

The Council, however, did not take the further step, to which it was urged by many both inside and outside the Church, of approving "the pill" or other chemical or mechanical methods of contraception. It taught responsible parenthood, but failed to rule on the methods to achieve it, or even to indicate whether it favored any easing of current rules. This it did in deference to an express request of Pope Paul, who made public the fact that Pope John had named a secret committee of experts to assemble and evaluate the facts and recommend to the pope such modification of existing rules as might seem appropriate. The names of 57 members, drawn from 25 countries of the 5 continents, were published in July 1964. Only 2 were bishops, and the 27 lay members included 3 married couples, a widow, and a single girl. All viewpoints, from the most conservative to the most advanced, were represented. It was reported in August 1965 that the committee had made an interim report to Pope Paul setting out certain elements on which its members were generally agreed. Up to the end of the Council, however, no announcement had been made by the pope. His only direct reference to the subject was a rather cryptic remark to an Italian newsman in October 1965. "The world wants to know what we think of birth control," he said, "and we must give an answer.

But what should it be? . . . The committees hold meetings, the mountains of reports and studies pour out. There is indeed no end to this study. But in the end, it is we who must decide. And at the moment of decision, we are alone. It is not as easy to decide as it is to study."[3]

While honoring the pope's request to leave the question of permissible methods of birth control in abeyance until the committee of experts had reported, the Council Fathers did make clear what they expected from the committee. Its first task, said Cardinal Suenens of Belgium, is "to study whether up to now we have given sufficient emphasis to all aspects of the teaching of the Church on marriage." In addition, he said, "It is for the commission to tell us whether we have excessively stressed the first end, procreation, at the expense of another equally important end, that is, growth in conjugal unity. In the same way, it is up to this commission to deal with the immense problem arising from the population explosion and overpopulation in many areas of the world. For the first time, we must proceed with such a study in the light of the faith. It is difficult, but the world, whether consciously or not, waits for the Church to express its thought and to be 'a light to the nations.'" Then, warning against the danger of a closed-mind approach that would fail to weigh adequately the new knowledge available in biology, psychology, and other modern sciences, he made a telling point. "I beg of you, my brother bishops,
* let us avoid a new 'Galileo affair.' One is enough for the Church." The applause that followed his speech revealed the extent to which other Fathers agreed.

Other speakers hammered home the same point. Patriarch Maximos IV Saïgh spoke of "a great crisis of the Catholic conscience. There is a question here of a break between the official doctrine of the Church and the contrary practice of the immense majority of Christian couples. The authority of the Church has been called into question on a vast scale. The faithful find themselves forced to live in conflict with the law of the Church, far from the sacraments, in constant anguish, unable to find a viable solution between two contradictory imperatives: conscience and normal married life."

The statement by Maximos Saïgh, confirmed by others, that

[3] *Corriere della Sera* (October 3, 1965).

great numbers of Christian couples use artificial means to prevent conception encouraged some theologians to affirm publicly
that a real doubt now exists in the Church as to whether there
is any morally significant difference between natural and artificial means of avoiding conception. To counter the suggestion
that Catholics were consequently free to make their own decisions, a group of conservatives made a last-minute attempt
to persuade Pope Paul to order the insertion of a clause in the
section on marriage reaffirming the condemnation of artificial
contraception contained in *Casti connubii*. After some bitter
infighting, a compromise was accepted by all parties. It condemned illicit practices, while leaving open the question as to
what practices were illicit. Catholics were also warned not to
use methods of birth control forbidden by the teaching authority of the Church, but in a context that left open the possibility of a change in current teaching by papal action on the
recommendations of the committee of experts.

Another notable contribution in the statement on the Church
in the Modern World is seen in its approach to atheism. Modern atheism is presented not only as a very complex problem
but one for which "believers themselves frequently bear some
responsibility." Too many theologians have tended to limit
Christianity to a strictly religious cult, affirming God to the
point of ignoring man and the world. Some philosophers have
reacted by stressing man and the world and ignoring or exclud-
ing God. Contemporary atheism is often primarily an affirmation of man and his function in the world, only indirectly a denial
of God as incompatible with man's freedom and initiative.

The remedy, the Council said, is to be sought in a proper
presentation of the Church's teaching. This requires "sincere
and prudent dialogue," as well as a common effort by all men
for the betterment of the world in which they live together.
Christians must, in addition, strive to remove the blemishes that
encourage the birth and growth of atheism. "To the extent that
they neglect their own training in the faith, or teach erroneous
doctrine, or are deficient in their religious, moral, or social
life, they must be said to conceal rather than reveal the authentic face of God and religion."

Many commentators have described the statement on the
Church in the Modern World as forming, with those on the

nature of the Church, on ecumenism, and on the liturgy, one of the Council's decisive contributions. The judgment has more validity for the statement's spirit than for its concrete achievements. It offers no specific solutions for the issues most agitating mankind. It neither bans the "bomb" nor blesses the "pill." Nevertheless, we see in the text a Church that is honestly trying to detach itself from its pedestal so that it can engage in fruitful discussion of mutually important issues on a basis of equality. As Protestant theologian and observer-delegate Oscar Cullmann summed it up, "It is not the letter of the texts that matters but the will to renewal that has led to their being drawn up at all."

Chapter 8

One Major Obstacle Remains

The antagonism between the Council and a powerful group within the Curia becomes more understandable when one remembers that the Curia is a development of the medieval papal government and court. Lacking institutions to express popular feeling, it became a self-perpetuating and self-regulating power structure. Its abuses have been a commonplace of Church history for a thousand years. The twelfth-century reformer, St. Bernard of Clairvaux, reserved for it what Pope Paul VI has called "burning pages." Every Council since Basle and Constance has sought to reform it, with no appreciable results. The Protestant Reformation received much of its stimulus from northern Europe's opposition to the Curia's bureaucratic and centralizing tendencies. The effect of the break was to tighten the curial grip on what remained.

Loss of the Papal States in the nineteenth century created among Catholics an emotional atmosphere that permitted a further concentration of control. To compensate for the papacy's shrinking temporal power, a policy of building up the personal popularity of the pope was inaugurated under Pius IX. It was he who started the custom of frequent public audiences. Bishops were summoned frequently to Rome to report to curial officials on their handling of the affairs of their dioceses, a practice formalized in the 1917 Code of Canon Law which obliges every European bishop to make the trip at 5-year intervals and other bishops at 10-year intervals.

The cult of the pope reached a peak after World War II. During the 1950 Holy Year, for example, millions of Catholics flowed into Rome to venerate the figure of "the gentle Christ on earth," as earlier generations of pilgrims had come to worship at the tombs of the Apostles. It was the cult of personality. Pilgrims applauded the pope, cheered him, photographed him in spite of the monopoly accorded to privileged curial photographers, pushed and jostled to touch the hem of his white soutane. The pope's face began to replace those of saints on medals. Theologians weighed his words as of more value for the determination of divine truth than the words of Scripture.

The Curia approved. What raised the pope's prestige and lowered that of the bishops was to its ultimate advantage. His civil servants smiled indulgently when a pope attempted to limit their powers. "Popes pass while the Curia remains," they would say. Or they would approvingly recall Pius XI's "I am too old" in reply to a cardinal who urged him to reform the Curia.

Pius XII did not think that he was too old. He decided that he could take on the Curia, and he formulated a plan that was audacious but not realistic. He believed that one man could control a centralized organization by reserving all decisions to himself. He was his own secretary of state. He built up a private secretariat in order to short-circuit curial offices. He reputedly planned a force of super cardinals to roam the world and oversee the execution by bishops everywhere of his directives.

But Pius XII never got that far. The Curia was too strong for him. It smothered him in detail, slowing down the decision-making process to a snail's pace. By his death in 1958, it had come to a practical standstill. Archbishop Thomas Roberts said at a press conference that when he was in Bombay, a decision on the validity of marriage could take ten years. And he added, "Who cares ten years later, even if the decision is favorable?"

The situation inherited by Pope John was, accordingly, a chaotic one. Having bigger fish to fry, however, John avoided a head-on collision. Instead, he invited the Curia's help, devoting much effort to winning its good will and restoring shattered morale. But he understood perfectly that curial reform was part of the total reform of the Church to which he was committed. He was equally satisfied that his predecessor's approach was self-defeating. John looked instead to the bishops to provide the counterweight. A restructuring of relations between them and the pope could transform the Curia into an administrative service controlled by the pope and subject to policies determined by the pope and the bishops.

A major defect of the Curia is that its institutions combine executive, administrative, and judicial powers without any clear division between these functions. The situation stems historically from medieval society in which the king both made laws and administered justice. While civil society has evolved organs of government both more sophisticated and more in keeping with human dignity, the Curia up to the time of the Council remained fossilized in its primitive forms.

The principal curial bodies are 12 ministries (called congregations), 3 courts, or tribunals, and 6 executive offices, plus 2 administrations to handle the property of the Holy See and Vatican finances. The total staff is about 500. This is the figure given by Alberto Cavallari, an Italian journalist who published a series of articles on the Curia in October 1965. In an unprecedented public-relations gesture, Cavallari was invited to study the whole operation and to interview the heads of departments as well as the pope. His verdict was that the Vatican was moving rapidly into the modern world in compliance with the directives given by the Council.

More significant, perhaps, than his verdict were the illustrations with which he documented his conclusions, for example his comments on what he saw in the pope's apartments. "It is quite amazing to see how radical are the updatings [*aggiornamenti*] even here. Red, for example, the traditional Catholic color . . . is no longer the color of the Vatican royal palace. . . . Everywhere we have the 'cold' colors which are favored today, from light greens to icy blues and champagne yellows. Such are the dominant themes, changing as one moves from one open room to the next, giving a sense of spaciousness."

Cavallari does not, however, claim that everything has changed. Of the Secretariat of State he wrote: "It is true that recruiting of staff is still Italian and remains within a framework of favoritism. Every pope and every cardinal brings in his own men. The secretariat has regional stratifications, a Venetian section, a Lombard section, an Emilian section, an Ancona section."[1] The Vatican yearbook confirms the Italian predominance in the Secretariat of State. More than four out of five names of some 120 staff members listed are Italian. The proportion is similar in other ministries.

The key ministry of the Curia is the Congregation for the Doctrine of the Faith, which was called the Supreme Sacred Congregation of the Holy Office before the reform announced by Pope Paul in December 1965. Set up in 1542 as the Sacred Congregation of the Roman and Universal Inquisition "to combat heresy," it has jurisdiction over all matters concerning faith and morals, that is to say, ultimately over everything within the competence and interest of the Church itself. It consequently retains authority in all the areas of specialized jurisdiction entrusted to other curial offices. It can interfere while a matter is pending before any of them, block a decision already announced, and issue a contrary one. It retains exclusive jurisdiction over important marriage cases, the publication and reading of books against the faith, and offenses against the unity of the Church such as heresy, schism, and apostasy.

Until December 1965 the Holy Office was investigator, prosecutor, judge, administrator, and executive rolled into one. Its proceedings took place in total secrecy. There was no prescribed form of trial for the accused person. He was often not even told he was being tried. His first notification might be condemnation and punishment, and it need not include the reason for the action. The victim frequently was obligated to keep secret the fact that he had been condemned and the reason for it (if he knew the reason).

Before the Council, few had any idea of the extent of the thought control exercised by the Holy Office. But when it began to forbid leading theologians to publish, for the benefit of the Council Fathers, their views on matters to be discussed, and banished them from Rome or forbade them to give talks to Council Fathers, groups of bishops decided that the interests of truth and of the Church demanded counteraction. Gradually it emerged that many perfectly orthodox writers were currently suffering arbitrary restraints, had lost their jobs, had their works

[1] *Corriere della Sera* (Milan, Italy, October 11 and 13, 1965).

suppressed, and were under a cloud with their superiors. Soon, in spite of Holy Office protests, many of these same theologians were being brought to Rome as advisers to the bishops—men like Yves Congar, Karl Rahner, Edward Schillebeeckx, and Hans Küng. They were to have their most cherished teachings enshrined in the decree on the nature of the Church and on ecumenism.

The issue became fully a matter of public record during the second session when, at a Council meeting, Cardinal Frings of Germany described the Holy Office procedures as a scandal. Cardinal Ottaviani snapped back that to attack the Holy Office was to attack the pope, in whose name it operated. But this defense had worn thin from much use. Others rallied to the support of Cardinal Frings, and it soon became obvious that the Holy Office had lost the confidence of the bishops.

Widespread approval, accordingly, greeted Pope Paul's issuance of a set of directives reforming the Holy Office, on December 7, 1965, the day before the Council closed. In addition to the already-mentioned change of name, the secrecy of its operation was ended. Theologians and others whose orthodoxy is called into question by the congregation's decisions will have the right to appeal and to be represented in judicial proceedings. A bishop must be consulted before a decision affecting one of his diocesans is made. At least two posts were abolished, the *commissario*, or judge, formerly called the "inquisitor," and the assistant who was in charge of censoring books. Finally, a body of consultors was set up, and closer liaison—in line with the Council's emphasis on the Scriptures—with the Pontifical Biblical Commission was recommended.

In addition to its right to interfere directly in the activities of the other curial offices, the Holy Office has traditionally kept a day-to-day control over them by a system of interlocking directorates. Even after its reform, Cardinal Ottaviani, its head, remains a member of nine other offices: the Consistorial (which names bishops all over the world), Religious Orders, Propagation of the Faith, Ceremonial, Extraordinary Affairs (which deals with governments), Seminaries and Universities, Court of the Apostolic Seal (the highest Roman tribunal), Bible Studies, and Interpretation of Canon Law. In addition, the first and second in command in all major offices, including the Secretariat of State, are members of the Holy Office. The Holy Office thus has the final word on all major decisions, the selection of nuncios and apostolic delegates, the naming of bishops and their promotion to key dioceses, education of the clergy, Vatican relations with foreign states, the drafting of texts to be issued as papal pronouncements.

Earlier chapters have recorded how this closely knit group was frequently able to frustrate the will of the Council majority. It was badly shaken in the first session by the unexpectedly strong support for Pope John's call for *aggiornamento*. But the Curia has a long history of successful resistance and a corresponding confidence in its ability to survive and triumph. Its comeback had reached impressive proportions by the time of the Council's final session. Dogged resistance to every proposal for modernization, ability to find points of division among progressives, ingenuity in introducing theological and political red herrings, and control of conciliar machinery had worn down the physical strength of the bishops and their willingness to fight. The final session was consequently marked by an anxiety on the part of the progressive leaders to disengage at whatever cost. They realized that a filibuster, such as had occurred at each of the three previous sessions, would gravely damage the prestige of the Council and the credibility of the Church. A decision could not be postponed for a year, as on the previous occasions, and they could hardly hope to rally the strength to smash a filibuster by direct action, at least not without a public scandal. Accordingly, they made every possible concession in the pending documents, accepting—for example—many ambiguities in the statement on relations with other religions and in that on religious freedom.

But the curial comeback was not confined to the Council documents. Of much greater concern was the postconciliar projection. There were already commissions to rewrite canon law, to continue liturgical reform, and to implement the decree on the communications media. A dozen other bodies were envisaged. They would threaten the Curia's autonomy unless it got control of them. Pope Pius IV had in 1564 set up a postconciliar commission to supervise the implementation of the decrees of Trent. It was quickly absorbed into the Curia; and as Cardinal Suenens of Belgium said at Vatican II, what then happened was very different from what the Council had decreed.

The synod of bishops, to be elected in large part by the national and regional conferences of bishops around the world, constituted the most direct threat. Even before the pope publicly announced the creation of the synod in September 1965, a series of incidents indicated a campaign to limit the impact of *Lumen gentium,* the conciliar decree that had proclaimed collegiality. Nuncios and apostolic delegates in various countries took steps to reassert curial control over the bishops. In the United States, the apostolic delegate warned the bishops not to implement the Council's approval of prayer in common with other Christians until Rome determined just how far they might go. His letter was represented as a directive from the pope himself. It soon emerged, however, that this was a curial formula. Everything a member of the Curia does is "on the instruction and by the authority of the Holy See."

Other communications from the apostolic delegate in Washington to various United States bishops reportedly urged them to curb certain vocal Catholic laymen with progressive views and to remove or keep laymen out of top editorial posts on Catholic newspapers. There followed an obedient flurry of episcopal criticisms of Catholic writers who had accepted the Mao-like invitations of the previous two years to "let all flowers bloom" and who had freely said what they thought. "There are being printed today Catholic publications which should not be found in Catholic homes," asserted Bishop Bernard Topel, of Spokane, Washington, in March 1965. "A coterie of Catholic writers specialize in denigrating priests," thundered Archbishop Joseph Hurley, of St. Augustine, Florida, who also heard "the characteristic intonation of the Communist voice in a few of our Catholic papers."[2] That was in May. In June, at the World Congress of the Catholic Press in New York, Cardinal Shehan of Baltimore chose a very inappropriate platform to deplore "the almost wholesale negative criticism which in recent years has been the almost constant stock-in-trade of some Catholic journals."[3]

[2] *Florida Catholic* (May 21, 1965).
[3] *The Catholic Journalist* (New York, July 1965).

Latin America reported similar efforts by nuncios. A quarter of a century ago, the decay of Latin American Catholicism shocked Rome into naming a number of enlightened and progressive bishops, men who by the time of Vatican II had reached positions of continent-wide respect and importance. The trend is now being reversed. Conservatives are being named to vacant sees, especially to the key places. The Curia, it would seem, places retention of control before the progress of religion. No opportunity is lost to downgrade and isolate progressive leaders.

Writing in the Flemish review *De Maand* in September 1965, Jan Grootaers saw the same pattern of efforts by the nuncios "to control and dominate the local Churches, at both the doctrinal and the ecumenical pastoral level." He mentions specifically Germany, Belgium, and the Netherlands, as well as the United States and Argentina. This factor may, he believes, be decisive in implementing the Council decisions. In other words, the reform voted by the Council cannot take effect unless and until the Curia is stripped of its usurped authority and made a civil service of the pope to carry out policy decided by the college of bishops with the pope at its head.

Pope Paul is well aware of the need to reform the Curia, and his modernization of Holy Office procedures is a significant first installment. His ideas, as developed in an address in September 1963 and on other occasions, suggest two main approaches, decentralization and internationalization. Decentralization, as he explained it, would place relations between the bishops and the Curia on a new basis, so that the Curia would no longer be "a pretentious and apathetic bureaucracy, narrowly legalistic and ritualistic, a hotbed of concealed ambitions and underhanded antagonisms, as some have charged," but "a true community of faith and charity" at the service of "the universal Church."

Decentralization would not spread the Curia itself around the world. It would restore to the individual bishops and to the national and regional bishops' conferences the powers absorbed by the Curia over the centuries. This is, of course, merely an application of the principle of subsidiarity, which Pope John, in *Mater et magistra,* followed Pius XI in calling "a fundamental principle of social philosophy, fixed and unchangeable." It is clear, in addition, that Pope Paul's thinking includes the further element of a change in the methods of formulating policy when he speaks of "a renewal of the relations between the bishops and the Curia." Instead of the chain of command presented by the Code of Canon Law, pope–curia–bishops, he would have the pope and bishops make the decisions and the Curia execute them. Accordingly, he proposed two measures. First, the bishops of various countries would "enter the council of the Roman congregations." Next, "if the Vatican Council should indicate a wish to do so, the bishops would be associated with the responsibilities of the Church." The Council took an early opportunity to put the bishops on record as wanting very much to share responsibility, and the pope then implemented his undertaking by creating the already mentioned synod of bishops.

Internationalization of the Curia is also important, and some progress has already been made. The progress has, nevertheless, been more statistical than real, and internationalization by itself is unlikely to cure the disease. Elites not only survive but flourish on controlled intake of outside talent. The Janizaries of the Ottoman Empire demonstrate this principle, as does the English upper class. Through the public schools and the Oxford and Cambridge universities, it has for centuries absorbed enough new blood in each generation to compensate for the normal deterioration of aristocratic inbreeding. The Roman Curia has long included men from other countries, and most such foreigners soon acquire the defects of the Italian members without their good qualities. They learn the rules but fail to assimilate the flexibility of manipulation that characterizes the true curialist.

Assuming, however, a proper restructuring of the lines of authority, the need for a full internationalization of the Curia would remain. The reason is not only the objective one which forced the United Nations to distribute its secretarial posts at all levels on a geographic-cultural basis, thus correcting the Western bias introduced in the first years before it had time to institutionalize itself. An additional historic reason exists. Centuries of Italian domination have established techniques of action and modes of thought that conflict hopelessly not only with those of the non-Western world but equally with the most important and dynamic sections of the West.

The issues had already been defined by the sixteenth century. Rome had fallen from its economic and cultural dominance. North and northeast of the Alps, in France and Germany, and later in England, the new civilization was taking shape. But Rome obstinately refused to yield its tattered historic claims to be the center of the universe. Instead, it concentrated on its narrow circle of achievement, despising what it could not emulate. It thus fostered the conditions for the initiation and the landslide success of the Protestant Reformation. Instead of learning from that disaster, it misinterpreted it to fit its prejudgments, and remained divorced from and in opposition to the positive elements in the French Revolution and the creation of the modern West.

Its misinterpretation of history was projected in due course across the Atlantic. For more than a century after the American Revolution, Rome regarded the United States as savage and uncouth, incapable of teaching Europe anything. The papal secretary of state thought it rather outrageous when the pope yielded to the evidence and, finally responding to a request initiated by Abraham Lincoln, appointed the first American cardinal in 1875.

Such traditions and attitudes have produced in the Curia, in the Italian Church, and even in Italian society a mentality that prevents an Italian-dominated administration from giving the service the Church needs and to which it is entitled.

René Laurentin gives an excellent example of the Roman mind. He deliberately goes back three centuries for this, demonstrating the total stability of the phenomenon. The head of the Inquisition, now the Holy Office, was then called the master of the sacred palace. R. Capisucchi, the incumbent in 1678 was —like most holders of the office about that time—opposed to the still-undefined doctrine of the Immaculate Conception of Mary, and he put on the Index of Forbidden Books an "Office of the Immaculate Conception approved by Pope Paul V." The decree carried the usual formulas. The book had been banned, it said, "by a special order of Pope Innocent XI, and after he had heard the views of the most eminent cardinals of the Inquisition."

All of that was words, the curial style as some would call it, pure invention in fact. But the author was more influential than the master of the sacred palace had realized. He was able to get the pope's ear, and Innocent XI supported the doctrine of the Immaculate Conception. So the curial wheels went into reverse in their own curious way. The master of the sacred palace headed a committee named to *revise* the condemned book. Some trivial and unsubstantial changes were made in the text, but not a word was deleted regarding the Immaculate Conception, the sole motive for the condemnation. In fact, the title of Immaculate Conception was introduced in two new places.

The author, accordingly, got substantial satisfaction. But the master of the sacred palace was not exposed for the arbitrariness and injustice of his original action. The condemned edition of the book stayed on the Index until Leo XIII's revision 200 years later.[4]

Many adjectives have been used to characterize the Roman mind. Michael Novak opts for the highly descriptive if awkward expression "nonhistorical orthodoxy."[5] It is, he says, a theology that rejects the two principles laid down by Pope John in *Pacem in terris* and in his opening address to the first session of Vatican II. Theologians and other thinkers who seek to analyze and judge contemporary events must, according to Pope John, enter the stream of history and work from inside it. They themselves and what they think and say are conditioned both by their own experience and that of previous generations. This is the principle of historical development. Any theory they elaborate or any answer they propose must meet the test of the situation for which they propose it. This is the principle of concrete reality.

The Roman mind has developed a philosophy to protect it against such principles. Called Scholasticism, it is a far cry from the thought of St. Thomas Aquinas and that of his mentor, Aristotle. Abandoning the data of experience, which these philosophers used as the foundation of their systems, the later Scholastics presented formulations in language that purported to be totally objective and consequently valid for all time and in every circumstance. It was an extremely interesting labora-

---

[4] *L'Enjeu du Concile: Bilan de la troisième session,* p. 352.

[5] *The Open Church: Vatican II, Act II* (New York, Macmillan, 1964), p. 183.

tory exercise. But it rested on a totally mistaken premise, namely, that the function of words is or can be to imprison thought, whereas they serve merely to achieve communication between minds.

From philosophy, the Scholastics in due course projected their error into theology. The result was the manuals of dogmatic theology, of moral theology, of casuistry, of canon law, of scriptural studies that long substituted for the educational process in Catholic seminaries all around the world. These manuals, learned mechanically and preferably verbatim by the students, provided ready-made answers for all possible questions, theoretical and practical. They placed the one who absorbed them in an impregnable tower, a bright, clear world of unchangeable truths. Inside the tower, it was legitimate to indulge in a game of speculation, an examination of the truths designed neither to challenge them nor to refine them but merely to confirm them. The investigator always knew the answer before he began. His function was to fill a few potholes on the road that led from his principles to the predetermined conclusion. Brilliancy consisted in finding a shorter or simpler road.

Practically every Father of the nearly 3,000 who attended Vatican II was raised in that school. In consequence, the Roman mind is not confined to Rome. Supporters in varying degrees were found among Fathers from every nation and continent, some—particularly from Spain and Latin America—who were totally encased in their ideological strait jacket, others whom contact with life had forced to make adjustments but who retained a greater or lesser part of their early formation.

The Council showed that such conditioning works not only on mediocre but also on brilliant minds. But it is not nearly so powerful as some have represented it. It makes a continuing and decisive impact only within countries where a disproportionate clerical influence has survived—Italy, Spain, parts of Latin America, Ireland. Even in those countries, as the Council voting showed time and again, it determines the total allegiance of a rather small minority of those exposed to it. Elsewhere, the continuing impact is marginal. The bishops of the United States were almost all trained in Roman universities in which they got high marks for their ability to absorb and project the typical manuals of theology or canon law. They so convinced their

Roman mentors of their "orthodoxy" that they were in due course selected by the Curia as men calculated to carry on its august traditions. Yet, with a handful of exceptions, when the chips were down at the Council, they recognized the absurdity of a position that claims the totality of truth, while—like Don Quixote with his helmet—refusing to subject it to the test of experience.

One must consequently recognize the critical part played by the controlled climate in which the members of the Curia are trained in order to understand why this body functions the way it does. Even in the United States, there is much criticism of the gap between the seminary regime and life in the twentieth century. In Italy, from which most of the Curia's members come, the gap is vastly wider. Seminarians in that country have traditionally been isolated from their families from the start of high school, or even earlier, until ordination. Only since World War II has it become common for them to spend one month's vacation a year in their homes, and even then they must wear a cassock.

Within the high walls of the institution that is their home, they are totally cut off from contact with the community, the city, and the world. They do not prepare for public examinations, and they follow courses of study equally cut off from the reality of the contemporary world as regards subject matter, teaching techniques, and textbooks. From this social and political vacuum, they pass directly to the seminary where, still isolated, they undergo the additional conditioning of Scholastic philosophy, theology, and canon law.

Those selected to enter the Curia then pass from one closed society into another. They lack the involvements and interests of their contemporaries raised in a world of dynamic and accelerating change. They have never learned to engage in a dialogue between equals. Having always been treated as children, they treat others as children. Having never been trusted, they do not know what trustworthiness is. When unchallenged, they tend to behave as dictators. When they are challenged, subterfuge and deception are the only weapons at their disposal.

Subterfuge and deception are qualities that deeply repel the modern world. Among history's many ironies, few are more cutting than the development in civil society, largely through pragmatic pressures, of a concept of truth more refined and exact than that practiced by Christ's followers. Rome's failure has been particularly humiliating. Cardinal Newman pointed to it more than a century ago. It caused him to hesitate, long after he had become convinced that the Church of Rome was the true Church of Christ.

No change of heart is yet visible. In defiance of Pope John's clear instructions that he wanted a Council without condemnations, the curialists who controlled the preparatory commissions presented to the Council a series of documents bristling with anathemas and calculated to embitter relations with other Christians. Time and again during the Council, members of the Curia were caught in misrepresentations or in misuse of their positions for partisan purposes, tactics that would have brought swift retribution if they were civil servants of any modern state. It was established that they altered the text of Council documents surreptitiously, and that they co-operated in distributing pamphlets containing scurrilous defamations of Council Fathers. A press release in October 1964 accused newsmen of having invented a letter that in fact had been sent to the pope by 17 cardinals.

The curialist position is that such dishonesty is not a failure in rectitude but simply stems from a different world view. It will not concede that candor is a virtue or that there can be reasons for making public what it is more convenient to conceal. What is more stupid, it will not face the fact that it is no longer possible to hide the unpleasant, that what it refuses to present in a good light will be subjected to public scrutiny under a hostile light.

The redoubtable Cardinal Ottaviani, head of the Curia and quintessence of its spirit, in an interview published on the eve of his 75th birthday (October 1965),[6] revealed the positive content that makes this tradition livable. "I am an old soldier," he said, "who serves the Church blindly." Here is precisely the mystique that forms the internal cement of the Curia. Its members see themselves as soldiers defending the beleaguered city from its enemies. Their tradition is that of the Swiss Guards.

[6] *Corriere della Sera* (October 27, 1965).

They will go down fighting rather than abandon their positions. One cannot but admire the cardinal's spirit when he insists that he has devoted his life to guarding the Church's treasure and that if the treasure changes (as a result of Council decisions), he will defend the new treasure with the same dedication as the old.

The position of the Curia and of Ottaviani himself, however, is not quite so simple. The cardinal begins by professing the blind obedience of the soldier, but when he speaks of protecting the "new" treasure, he adds an unsoldierly condition. It must be a treasure *in which he believes*. And he throws in a further, quite unsoldierly, comment. "If you tell an old soldier that the laws have been changed," he says, "it is clear that he reacts as an old soldier and does everything in his power to prevent their being changed." This is similar to the spirit of a general in the Spanish or Latin American tradition who chooses a military dictatorship rather than accept the democratization of the regime. Here is the ambivalence of the Curia, its confusion of policy and policing. Its members are old soldiers who execute orders with soldierly thoroughness, but only the orders they approve.

In addition to its internal cohesion, the system based on the Roman mind has powerful external supports. The main identifiable power structures that support the Curia for their own ends are small but wealthy and highly cohesive reactionary groups in Italy, Spain, and—strangely enough—France. The ones that have been most publicized are the Italian Neo-Fascist groups whose mouthpiece is the scurrilous *Il Borghese,* and the less extreme right-wing elements reflected by *Il Tempo.* But Spain has similar aristocratic groupings. They lean heavily on the curialized Church to retain their privileged place in society. Their great fear is a progressive clergy that would back the insistent demands of the workers for a voice in their country's life.

In France, the reactionaries are held together largely by nostalgia. It affects the descendants of the pre-Revolutionary aristocracy, revives memories of the conflict between constitutionalist and anticonstitutionalist priests formally resolved by Napoleon's Concordat, picks up support among the ultramontane extremists outraged by Pius IX's efforts to reach a working agreement with the anticlerical Third Republic. In this century, these forces rallied around the Action Française movement between the two World Wars. Later they found a new cause in Algeria, challenging the authority of France and outraging the conscience of humanity by the barbaric methods of their "crusade" to prevent Algerians from exercising a clearly expressed political choice.

Their opposition to the reforms sought by the Council majority has been equally self-righteous and ruthless. They have demonstrated in churches and cathedrals in France to prevent addresses by "liberals" invited by bishops to discuss the Council. Their lobby in Rome has been less violent in expression but equally intransigent in position. Its principal organ was a group that called itself Roc (rock) and that gave lectures in a hall a few doors from the Holy Office. A favorite whipping boy was—logically—Teilhard de Chardin. Henri Rambaud, for example, employed a long hour of diatribe to reach the conclusion that "between 1916 and 1919, Teilhard changed his religion. He may have always wished to remain a Christian, but he no longer knew what Christianity was." Father Philippe de la Trinité, consultor to the Holy Office, was no less devastating. The teaching of Teilhard, he proclaimed, "is an evolutionist modernism of a cosmo-religious type, placed under the sign of a vague Pan-Christism."

Similar marriages or concubinages of convenience between the Roman mind and reactionary groups exist in various parts of Latin America. Archbishop Geraldo de Proença Sigaud, of Diamantina, Brazil, for example, openly identified himself both in Rome and in Brazil as opposed to the Johannine *aggiornamento* and the major reforms voted by the Council. In nearby Uruguay, Catholics demonstrated in June 1965 against the papal nuncio and the apostolic administrator of Montevideo on the ground that they were blocking the Council reforms that other Uruguayan dioceses were already implementing. The government of Uruguay also protested to the Vatican against improper activities of the nuncio, and he was withdrawn. Meanwhile, in Mexico a group styling itself the Mexican Traditionalist Movement, and claiming association with like movements in the United States, spent massive sums on advertisements protesting the Vatican Council reforms. Some bishops at first encouraged it, but withdrew support after a strong denunciation by the archdiocese of Mexico City.

It is in Italy itself, however, that the politico-religious alliance is most solidly institutionalized. Both parties have the same concrete need. Minorities left behind by the flow of history, they need a myth to retain their cohesion and sustain their drive. For several centuries, they claimed that the Protestant Reformation had caused all the ills of the Church and of society. By the twentieth century, however, Catholic-Protestant relations had so evolved that the explanation was wearing thin. In its place we now have the myth of Communist responsibility for whatever is not as it should be in the Church and in the world. Since the Neo-Fascists and other right-wing groups in Italy find in the same line justification for their existence, a perfect working partnership exists.

The temptation to use the Church as a political force has deep roots in Italy. When the Papal States were absorbed into the kingdom of Italy in 1870, the Vatican forbade Catholics to participate in elections. The prohibition was gradually relaxed in the early twentieth century in efforts to halt the progress of the Socialist Party, founded in 1892. After World War I, the Vatican threw its support to Don Sturzo's Popular Party. During the 1920s it switched to Mussolini, who in 1929 regularized relations between the Vatican and Italy by the Lateran agreements and a concordat.

A plebiscite in 1946 substituted a republic for the monarchy, and two years later a constitution was promulgated. Although it guaranteed the democratic process, the decisions continued to be made by the old power structures: the Church, big business, financial monopolies, and bureaucratic civil service. The masses remain underrepresented, in part because of low levels of education, in part because of a lack of identification of the individual Italian with the nation. The republic has consequently been characterized by unstable governments and a continuing drift of discontented voters toward the political Left.

The Curia and the Italian bishops have concentrated on checking this drift not by changing the conditions that encourage it but by trying to persuade Italian Catholics that the political Left is their enemy. The same line is sedulously peddled by the spokesmen of the Right. They glorify Pius XII as the leader of the anti-Communist forces and denounce John XXIII and the majority of the Council Fathers for having opened the floodgates of destruction by postulating a possible position for the Church and the world other than doctrinaire anti-Communism.

One point that emerges clearly is that curial positions reflect not only theological beliefs but vested interests. A combination of motives produces the tortuous reasoning by which members of the Curia persuade themselves that, acting in the name and on the authority of the pope, they should oppose the pope when they decide that he is acting against their concept of the good of the Church.

Church reform, as Pope John clearly recognized and as Pope Paul has insistently repeated, requires reform of the Curia. The vastness of the task is to be measured by the many layers of obstacles encrusted on that venerable body. Because of their ignorance of human ways, the members of the Curia shrink from contacts of equality with their fellow Christians. The worship of their own petty authority blocks the willing acceptance of the principle of decentralization of authority, still more the downgrading to their proper status as a civil service. And beyond that is the vast financial structure that binds Vatican policy to Italy's financial circles and industrialists, the political Right.

While Vatican II has no more than begun the process of curial reform, its contribution should not be minimized. In the decree on the office of bishops, it went on record as desiring the reorganization of the curial departments and their adaptation to the needs of the times, regions, and rites, especially as regards their number, name, competence, and peculiar method of procedure, as well as the co-ordination of work among them. It also asked a clarification of the functions of papal representatives and a true internationalization of all curial offices.

Perhaps even more important, Vatican II made possible the open discussion within the Church of the Curia and its defects. November 8, 1963, the day Cardinal Frings of Germany told the assembled Fathers that the proceedings of the Holy Office were "a scandal," was a red-letter day in the history of Church reform. Curial abuse, like abuse in other civil services, thrives on secrecy. And, as Cardinal Cushing of Boston has said, public opinion within the Church is "an essential part of its existence as an institution." The opening up of the Curia to the impact of informed public opinion gives the best assurance that its methods and functions will be adjusted to serve the needs of the Church of our time.

Chapter 9

The Real
Work Begins

Historians may indeed decide that open discussion within the Church was the decisive gain registered by Vatican II. Without it, nothing would have changed. The Council would have been an assembly in the totalitarian mold, and would never have stirred the interest and hopes of the world. Suddenly, instead of the familiar monolith, the Roman Catholic Church was seen as a living association of 500 million humans with their own minds, their own aspirations. The approving reaction of world opinion was instantaneous. People everywhere sensed that all mankind would benefit from the results of a self-examination by the Catholic Church conducted openly and honestly. From that moment, the world was sympathetically committed to the purposes of the Council and the interests of the Church.

There is no going back on this gain. Pragmatically, it would be folly to do so. Open discussion has established its value as a catalyst of the latent energies in the Church. In addition, it represents an acceptance of the social realities of the twentieth century.

The next step is to develop institutions to facilitate the methodical formation and expression of public opinion in the Church, as has occurred in civil society. This may cause a conflict within the Church as sharp as that experienced in civil society in the fight for a free press in the eighteenth and nineteenth centuries. Such at least is the prognosis from the tentative efforts that have been made in the United States to transform a few Catholic publications from house organs of the hierarchy into voices of the people of God. But there is no alternative. To clamp down again on the expression of opinion, to attempt to restore the monolithic controls of the past, could only result in a massive loss of the Church's most dynamic elements. A dramatic exodus in the form of a schism is unlikely. Today's social conditions would favor, rather, an unspectacular but catastrophic drifting away.

If the principles established at the Council are taken seriously, what changes should one anticipate in the Catholic Church in the United States?

They will not be small changes. In many respects they will be more far-reaching than those set forth by Martin Luther in the famous theses which sparked the Reformation. So distinguished a Protestant spokesman as Bishop Otto Dibelius of Berlin publicly declared that if the Catholic Church had in the sixteenth century given the response that Vatican II has now given, the Reformation would not have been necessary.

As the liturgical reform progresses, further changes in the forms of worship will be introduced. There will be a growing stress on the Bible, more reading of the Scriptures at prayer meetings, more explanation of the Scriptures in sermons. There will be a parallel stress on the community aspects of worship, a trend to smaller church buildings to encourage active participation of the faithful, a relocation of altars to promote a union of priest and people in the Eucharistic liturgy. Novenas to the Miraculous Medal and to St. Jude and other private devotions will be de-emphasized. As far as possible they will be incorporated as subsidiary elements in the official prayer of the Church.

Rules for day-to-day living and practice will likewise change. There will be a withdrawal from casuistic determinations of what work is permissible on Sundays, when meat may or may not be eaten, and when and how fasting should be undertaken. Obligations will be presented more positively. The area of discretion and judgment for the individual will be broadened.

This more adult role for the layman will extend to the running of the Church. Forms of government will move closer to those usual in other Churches in America, not only because of ecumenical pressures but because these will better reflect the new reality within Catholicism. The lay role in Church finances and education will grow. Clerical garb will be simplified, and the physical and psychological barriers between clergy and laity will be lowered. Modifications of the worker-priest concept will probably appear, as Catholic clergymen borrow from some recent American Protestant initiatives in which ministers live among the poor on their own level. Even monasteries and convents may pull down their massive walls and throw open their gardens as parks and children's playgrounds. Priests and nuns will cease to make headlines when they follow their consciences in a direction not approved by their superiors, because they will no longer seem either disobedient or unusual.

If one seeks a factor common to these changes, they all seem to follow logically from the Council's upgrading of the dignity of the human person, its concern for human rights in the enlarged sense in which these are understood by contemporary man.

Catholic apologists like to claim for Christianity a decisive role in the identification and proclamation of human rights. Admittedly, the teaching of Christ as embodied in the Gospels and in Christian literature provides a foundation for these concepts. Nor is it unreasonable to claim that Christianity started cultural trends in Europe, out of which historically grew the notions today proclaimed in (for example) the declarations and conventions of the United Nations.

It is, however, no less true that the Catholic Church often failed to act on its principles. The Church was the patron of education, but could never project education beyond the elite. In consequence, it trapped itself in the false dichotomy of a ruling class and inert masses in both the civil and religious spheres. Not the Church but the secular world first demonstrated that universal education could become a reality, that free speech did not necessarily degenerate into anarchy, that religion could thrive in independence from the state. Similarly, the antislavery movement, if Christian in principle, found its main support outside the Catholic Church. The emancipation of women is equally a triumph of the secular world, one that the Church is still far from accepting emotionally or implementing institutionally. And even something so totally Christian as the ecumenical movement grew up under the inspiration of the Holy Spirit outside the Catholic Church and was long bitterly opposed by its spokesmen.

Belatedly but sincerely, Vatican II faced such unpalatable facts. It was important to do so. The Church's previous insistence that it was always right had constituted an insuperable obstacle to dialogue with other Christians and with the world. Accordingly, it was a decisive breakthrough when the Council went on record, in the statement on religious freedom, that "in the life of the people of God, as it has made its pilgrim way through the vicissitudes of human history, there has at times appeared a way of acting that was hardly in accord with the spirit of the Gospel and even opposed to it."

In more concrete ways, too, the Council expressed its recognition of the values of the human person. The decision to introduce the vernacular in the Mass reflects it. The reasons for using the vernacular were equally strong when Luther made his demands four centuries earlier, but the Church's leaders were then less conscious of the rights of the rank and file. The liturgy decree also places a new stress on the service of the Word, formerly played down in the Catholic Mass in favor of the sacramental liturgy. The function of the word is to facilitate communication, and communication is between persons. Even the sacrament of the Eucharist is being increasingly explained in terms of a personal encounter with Christ.

In the statement on religious freedom, the dignity of the person is the whole basis of the exposition. "The right to religious freedom has its foundation in the very dignity of the human person," says the statement, ". . . not in the subjective disposition of the person but in his very nature." The first chapter of the statement on the Church in the Modern World is devoted to analyzing the dignity of the human person, evaluating from a different viewpoint the ideas of the statement on religious freedom. "Only in freedom can man direct himself toward goodness. . . . Man's dignity demands that he act according to a knowing and free choice that is personally motivated and prompted from within." The new theology of marriage formulated in the same statement has a similar basis. It firmly asserts the primacy of the personal elements, the autonomy within the moral law of the husband and wife acting as responsible persons.

The incorporation of the principle of human dignity in a series of Council documents, however, does not mean that it has now become part of the currency of the Church. Nor will the changes outlined before, as logically following from the decisions of the Council, occur automatically. It cannot even be assumed that the bishops back home will want to pursue the policies they espoused in Rome. It is true that they established for themselves at the Council the right to open discussion. The proclamation of collegiality and the creation of a synod of bishops prepared the way for them to participate in the Church's decision-making processes. But, as English historian E. E. Y. Hales has pointed out, the wresting of Magna Carta from King John by the barons brought no quick benefit to the commoners. On the contrary, the petty local tyrant often proved a harsher ruler than the distant monarch had been.[1]

Even during the Council, many commentators noted the paradox of bishops who made bold decisions in Rome but moved with extreme caution in implementing them at home, who spoke daringly in St. Peter's but were outraged when people in their own dioceses repeated the same ideas. Such ambivalence can be expected. While we have in principle a substitution of a new concept of concentric circles in Church organization, in practice we have no more than a broadening of the seat of authority at the summit of the ecclesiastical pyramid. And while the bishops were perfectly happy to have more power placed in their hands, many of them know how to exercise it only in the same arbitrary way in which they themselves were formerly subject to it.

If the bishops need prodding, who is going to prod them? The unfolding of the reform movement during both the preparatory period and the Council itself indicates that the task will fall mainly to the *periti,* that small group of priests who served as advisers to the bishops in theology, Scripture, sociology, canon law, and a host of allied subjects. They come from many countries, belong to different orders and to the diocesan clergy. Before the Council they suffered in obscurity for their convictions, but have now become famous. A network of professional

[1] *Pope John and His Revolution* (New York, Doubleday, 1965), p. 198.

reviews permits rapid world-wide exchange of views among them. The Council brought them together in bonds of personal friendship. Today they are eagerly sought by the highest institutions of Catholic learning, and publishers compete for their writings.

Nevertheless, many within the ranks of their fellow clergy are uneasy about the influence of these newly famous *periti*. This is partly explained by the fact that Vatican II stressed the importance of the bishop, and spoke of the layman as a member of the people of God. The unintended effect, at least psychologically, was to downgrade the lower clergy. When priests began to protest, the Council decided to devote a separate document to the priesthood, which it described, however, in terms significantly different from those used when speaking of the Church. There the Fathers had stressed the priest's participation in the office of Christ through the ministry of the Word, leadership in the sacramental liturgy, and spiritual guidance of his flock. The decree on the priesthood returns to the pre-Council emphasis on the priest as the one who offers the Eucharistic sacrifice in the name of the whole Church. It also speaks at length of the priest as delegate of the bishop, and of the authority he enjoys within the hierarchy of the Church. These aspects of the priestly office have been given great prominence in modern devotional literature, particularly in the United States, as being calculated to ensure respect for the priest and give him an aura of untouchability to sustain him in his celibate life. Recent theologians fear that this attitude tends to deform the notion of the Christian priesthood as presented in the Scriptures and in the early Church. Their view, which influenced the Council's description of the priest in the document on the nature of the Church, is that the priest should not be pictured as the intermediary between God and man but as the leader of his people in their dealings with God.

The Council's own conflicting motivations in these two documents give an idea of the range of attitudes within the ranks of the clergy toward the whole program of change voted by the Council. Institutional pressures are strongly negative, and added to them is the personal resistance flowing from a seminary education completely out of sympathy with the mind of the Council. Yet there is also a strong sense of loyalty and highly developed if not highly motivated obedience. The clergy may not obey gladly, but if they are pushed hard enough, they will obey. Finally, there is a growing awareness that the traditional methods are not working, that the Church must update to renew contact with modern man.

In the United States, the number of young priests and nuns who are impressed by the pastoral need to update is substantial. Many of them have even made the emotional transformation and see themselves as involved in a family-type relationship with the laity, not the dominant element in a dichotomy. They seek involvement in what concerns the society around them, in civil rights, peace movements, academic freedom, and questioning of traditional values.

This ferment of change has reached the seminaries. In the United States, as elsewhere, these institutions provide a program of studies and personal formation little changed since the Council of Trent. They proved successful in restricting the sixteenth-century expansion of Protestantism, but they have shown themselves much less able to meet the challenge of the Humanist culture that has dominated Western society for over a century. The Council in its statement on the Church in the Modern World urged incorporation into Catholic thinking of all the positive elements in Humanism, and seminaries are starting to feel the need to do this, particularly in the United States, where many seminarians were exposed to the general culture in their earlier education. In a statement on the training of priests, the Council also advised that before starting ecclesiastical studies, candidates "should be equipped with the humanistic and scientific training which young men in their own countries are wont to have as a foundation for higher studies." However, both in this document and in one dealing with education in general, the Council introduced an emphasis in favor of retaining the traditional atmosphere in Catholic schools and seminaries. This ambivalence adds to current tensions.

The reassessment of the priesthood begun by Vatican II has opened discussion on a subject previously taboo, the priest's obligation of celibacy. Following the example of Christ and the urging of the Scriptures, the Church has always extolled voluntary celibacy. It early became obligatory for monks and nuns. The Eastern Churches do not allow a priest to marry, but they ordain married men, who then continue to live with their wives.

The subject is one of particular delicacy in the United States. Celibacy had popularly become regarded as so intimately associated with the character of the Catholic priest that in 1928 the American bishops had Rome extend the law to priests of the Eastern rites. Since that time, such priests have been bound by the law of clerical celibacy if they exercise their ministry in the United States. During 1965, nevertheless, it became clear that opinion was not as monolithic on this subject as had formerly seemed the case. Discussions in learned articles and books were reinforced by a lengthly correspondence in the *National Catholic Reporter*, a weekly newspaper published in Kansas City by a group of Catholic laymen. It established that substantial sentiment exists among both priests and laymen that priestly celibacy should be a free option, not a requirement for exercising the pastorate.

The first mention of clerical celibacy at the Council was an appeal by various bishops for more humane treatment of priests who had found their commitment to celibacy beyond their strength. No official acknowledgment was made of these requests, but Rome introduced new administrative procedures. Requests for permission to marry were no longer automatically rejected. A priest may be returned to the lay state, which means that he cannot exercise his priestly functions; after that, he may also be authorized to marry. Exceptions have also been made in a few cases for Protestant clergymen who had become Catholics; after being ordained to the Catholic priesthood, they have been authorized to perform priestly duties while continuing to live with their wives. One such permission was given by Pope John in early 1962, just before the Council opened.

Some priests wanted to go further. In June 1965, for example, a two-day reunion was held by priests representing the seven dioceses of the city and province of Buenos Aires, Argentina. The meeting was attended by two bishops and addressed by several theologians. The 80 priests present recommended the ending of compulsory celibacy. They did so, they said, not only because of the personal problems of many priests, but because the single priest was often less equipped than a married one to deal with problems encountered in today's ministry.

A Brazilian bishop, Peter Paul Koop, wanted the Council to

voice an opinion. He prepared a statement in which he asserted that the Church in Latin America could not meet its need for priests unless it ordained married men as part-time priests. "We have to make a choice right away: either to multiply the number of priests both celibate and married, or look forward to the collapse of the Church in Latin America." The intervention, however, was never presented to the Council. At Pope Paul's request, it was decided not to air the issue. Those who had opinions were asked to submit them privately to the pope.

Discussion has, nevertheless, not been stifled among Catholics, and this is a measure of the reality of change within the Catholic community. While nearly all priests still regard a papal request as a command, educated laymen are more fully members of a twentieth-century society in which expression of unofficial opinion is considered essential to the proper functioning of government. One can predict that the matter will not be left to rest in a Vatican pigeonhole.

There are at least two reasons why the laity are more open to change than the clergy. As we have seen, the effect of the Council was to lessen the importance of the priest and stress the role of the laity in the Church. In addition, by reason of their education and daily work the laity are more exposed to contemporary culture, and are consequently more conscious of the need to revise archaic structures if the Church is to survive and flourish.

There are other forces, nevertheless, which cause a significant number of lay people to fear the new directions proposed by the Council. Emphasis in Catholic instruction has long been on the unchangeability of the Church's teaching, with little effort to distinguish the essential from the peripheral. The accompanying sense of security in a world characterized by the acceleration of change has been, for many, one of the major values derived from their membership in the Church. The continuance of a Counter Reformation mentality has so stressed the errors of non-Catholics that changes are sometimes seen simply as efforts to "Protestantize" the Church, even if what is involved is simply the greater use of English in the Mass, a more active participation of the congregation in worship, the singing of hymns, and readings from the Scriptures.

Among such people, however, there is no strong intellectual

conviction to maintain a cohesive body of resistance to liturgical and other changes. The experience of the Council itself was that the solidly convinced opposition to the principle of *aggiornamento* was as low as 2 or 3 per cent of the bishops, the few higher negative votes reflecting tactical allegiances for specific objectives. The intellectually convinced opposition in the entire Church membership is probably no higher proportionately than it is among the bishops. However, resistance is understandably much greater among ordinary Catholics who have not shared the exposure to, and discussion of, the new ideas experienced by the bishops in Rome.

Two things are accordingly clear: The Council has in fact laid the groundwork for major changes in the Catholic Church, and there are strong forces within the Church both for and against implementation of these changes. In the circumstances, the stand of the pope becomes of critical importance, at least for the short and medium term. One pope opened a window; could not another close it? Pius IX had begun his pontificate with an expansive gesture of friendship toward a world with which he would find himself in hopeless conflict 20 years later. Could that history not repeat itself?

It was certainly evident, as the bishops scattered to the four corners of the globe after the final curtain had rung down on Vatican II, that the seat of power still rested firmly in Rome. The very documents intended to increase the participation of the bishops in the Church's decision-making processes insisted that they did not diminish papal authority. It was also abundantly clear that many in the Curia were impatiently awaiting the withdrawal of the "barbarians" to revive their eclipsed intransigence.

Where, then, does Pope Paul stand? The answers cover the entire spectrum. "So conservative that if he had followed Pius XII immediately, nobody would have noticed the difference," some believe. "Totally dedicated to the letter and spirit of Pope John's *aggiornamento*," others claim.

The comparison with his immediate predecessors is inevitable. As a man, he is obviously closer to the ascetic and intellectual Pius XII. His life was spent even more fully than that of Pius within the confines of the Vatican, in a cloister of ciphers and secrets. Except for some months as a junior secretary in

Warsaw, he never worked outside Italy. He lacked any experience to compare with John's 28 years in Bulgaria, Turkey, Greece, and France. Even his eight years as archbishop of Milan did little to humanize his manner. His polish is total, yet he lacks spontaneity. Every word is weighed, every gesture measured.

To say that he is not John is to repeat the obvious, but to make it a criticism is an injustice. John was a unique blessing, a gratuitous gift to the world. To set him up as a standard against which to judge other popes makes no sense. What is more pertinent is that John in his lifetime believed that Montini—whom he made a cardinal—could be relied upon to complete his reform of the Church. Significant also is the fact that the whole world breathed a sigh of relief when the cardinals chose Montini to follow John, in an atmosphere that indicated a desire to continue John's policies.

But has Paul as pope matched the trust placed in him by John and by those who approved of John's ideas? Many think he has not. Certainly he has managed to keep everyone guessing, to straddle the fence so successfully as to leave a doubt regarding his own preferences. In addition, he revealed personal attitudes annoying to the progressive majority at the Council. Specifically, he continually showed an exaggerated concern—what some have called an obsession—with the prestige of the office of pope. At no time in history was the world more conscious of the pope's power. The Fathers at the Council, while seeking to clarify episcopal authority, were scrupulously careful to avoid any suggestion that they were doing so at the expense of the papacy. But Paul never seemed satisfied. The decree on the Church emerged with the "explanatory note" presenting the pope's independence of action in terms—which the bishops had been at pains to avoid—that suggested the possibility of a conflict. When the Fathers decided not to insert the new title of "Mother of the Church" in the conciliar statement on Mary, Paul picked the ceremony of promulgation of that document to confer on her, on his own authority, the same title. Again and again, he seemed to assert claims that the bishops had not challenged.

Only second to his concern for the prestige of his office was Paul's anxiety to placate the minority. This was particularly evident during the Council's third session, the session of the "explanatory note" and of the 19 last-minute changes in the decree on ecumenism presented in circumstances showing scant respect for majority rights. But when the spokesmen of the majority urged the pope to permit action on the drafts on religious freedom and on the Jews, he would not force the minority to stop the behind-the-scenes maneuvers by which they were keeping these documents from reaching the floor.

One might judge Paul's concern for the minority excessive and yet hardly criticize his anxiety to avoid showdowns. And in the end, he did not give much of substance to the minority. Toward the close of the third session, the tail seemed to be wagging the dog. Many were saying in public that the Council's high hopes were dashed. But in its final session, the Council exceeded all reasonable anticipations. If there was no document that could not have been better, neither had any of them been essentially vitiated. And this had been done without a widening of the gap between the conflicting parties. Pope Paul might reasonably feel that he had executed his trust faithfully.

To his fingertips Paul is a Roman diplomat. He will not say or do anything that will commit him further than a given situation seems to require. He regards his flexibility of action and ambiguity of decision as a major asset. And indeed it is just that. The successful conclusion of the Council is a tribute to his ability to carry water on both shoulders.

Yet events ultimately compel decisions. Successful diplomacy and war alike call for a firm stand at the right moment. And the immediate postconciliar period will produce many situations requiring a firm stand. The conciliar minority survives and will be heard from. "We must expect a wave of conservatism in the postconciliar Church," according to Father François Houtart, Belgian sociologist and expert at the Council. "This is perfectly normal when one considers the effect of social change within a group. It could even be, at some points, quite an aggressive phenomenon."

A crucial issue is, of course, the control of the Roman Curia. It is the one seat of power in the Church totally out of tune with the spirit of Vatican II and decisively opposed to the reform voted by the Council. Throughout the world, as we have seen, there are some powerful individuals and even some groups with similar attitudes. But without the Curia, they would be like the Japanese holdouts on Pacific atolls after World War II. The pope's stand on curial reform will consequently determine the extent of his true commitment to the updating of the Church.

Having spent his lifetime in the Curia, Paul is better placed than most to understand it. And he is more firmly on the record than any of his predecessors on the need for reform. But it is equally obvious that he is keenly aware that the pope needs the Curia. He is determined not to repeat Pius XII's mistake. Consequently, his concrete approaches to implementing reform have been cautious to the point of timidity. Paul's first step was an appeal to the Curia in September 1963 to reform itself, a step followed by the naming of an internal committee to draft a program of self-reform. The one significant result by the end of the Council was the reorganization of the Holy Office. This represents a major advance. Coupled with the public rehabilitation for the first time in history of persons censured by the Holy Office, it eliminates one of the Curia's most deadly weapons. But it leaves the institution intact. When the Inquisition became the Holy Office, it lost some of its coercive powers. But it managed to get along impressively without them.

Pope Paul marshals the pros and cons of each problem, neatly balancing reasons for and against. It is a characteristic so pronounced that it has earned him the name of "the pope of buts." While recommending self-reform to the Curia, he defends it stoutly against outside critics. Nepotism and simony are things of the past, he told an Italian newsman in late 1965.[2] "Some technical reforms are undoubtedly required to improve its work, but that creates no serious problems." Shortly afterward, he expanded the same ideas in an address to the Council, praising the Curia's "religious spirit, the sincere love of Jesus Christ, the fidelity and obedience, the zeal for the good of the Church, and the haste to promote its progress." At the same time, he added, he agreed with the Council's request for improvement. The studies already made had satisfied him that there was no great need for structural reforms. There would be some modi-

[2] Alberto Cavallari, whose interview with Pope Paul appeared in *Corriere della Sera* (Milan, October 3, 1965).

fications, simplifications, and improvements. Guiding principles would be better formulated and established. The transformation "will seem slow and partial, and so it should because of the respect which the persons and traditions merit."

If this were the only evidence on record, one might wonder if the Pauline reform was not destined for the same fate as the many that preceded it, thereby confirming the Roman saying that popes pass but the Curia remains. But one other favorable, hopefully decisive, factor must be introduced. This is the synod of bishops.

Pope Paul, it will be recalled, made many unhappy in January 1965 by increasing the number of cardinals in circumstances which suggested that the expanded college would be the "senate" he had told the bishops they could have if they wished. Some months later, however, he did in fact set up a new body to be elected in large part by the world's bishops. Here is an instrument which the pope can use to keep the Curia under control, and which the bishops can use to see that he does so. In isolation, the pope is in all truth "the prisoner of the Vatican." The bishops are the ones who can free him.

Probably even more decisive than the creation of the synod of bishops is a result that has been achieved by the Council at the noninstitutional level. This is the already mentioned release of internal dynamism, the spontaneous explosion of the power of the spirit, expressing itself in a public opinion previously almost unknown in the Church. Here is what is really new as a result of Vatican II. It is a force that can work decisively with Pope Paul to complete curial reform and Church updating, if, as it seems, this is his ultimate purpose. And even if his heart is not fully in the task, as some still fear, or if he really conceives it in the superficial terms in which he at times voices his purposes, one can hope that the new force will prove so strong as to carry him to the end of the path he has taken.

Pope John convened the Council, it must be remembered, not simply to update the Church for the benefit of its members. He wanted changes that would open the way to unity among Christians and that would help the cause of peace by enabling the secular world to talk again with the Catholic Church, to see their common interests, and to work together for their common objectives.

Enough has been said to indicate that significant progress has been made toward the restoration of Christian unity. Many emotional obstacles have been swept away and concrete measures of association have been taken. There is a realistic understanding on all sides that amalgamation of the institutions and governing bodies of the major Christian Churches is not even ripe for discussion. But both Catholics and other Christians agree that a continuation of the lines of internal change begun in the Catholic Church by the Council will bring the day of full reunion nearer.

The Council's other proclaimed purpose—to bridge the chasm that separates the Church from the Humanist culture of the twentieth century—fared less well. The deliberations of the Council itself were devoted almost entirely to the internal concerns of the Church as an institution. In addition, the method of conducting the deliberations showed scant concern for the effect on the watching world. Much that the bishops did seemed to lack humility, honesty, and simplicity. Gestures were often substituted for deeds. Respect for persons rated higher than principle.

The statement on the Church in the Modern World was intended by the Council to be its formal approach to contemporary culture, its idea of how it conceived the world in which men actually live, its suggestion of how the Church can and should contribute to the betterment of this world and the solution of such pressing problems as ignorance, hunger, and war. But the content of the statement, for all its positive value, fell short of being meaningful to those to whom it was directed. It was, rather, an effort to establish an internal consensus preliminary to debate, a working paper by Catholics for Catholics.

It is only in a historical perspective, therefore, that it is possible to pass a judgment on the success of Vatican II. One must admit that the Council did not accomplish all it set out to do. But one may fairly claim that it did as much as could reasonably be expected. The Fathers faced up realistically to the threat that human society was moving forward on a course of its own and leaving the Church behind in an irrelevant backwater. They recognized that the course of society was irreversible and that the duty of the Church was to adjust, not to resist.

The immediate challenge to its members, accordingly, is to prepare themselves to live in a society in which Christians will not be Christians by custom and tradition, but only by a personal faith attained in a difficult struggle and perpetually renewed. Major effort must thus be devoted to opening up seminaries and other Catholic educational establishments to the social, political, and cultural advances of the times. The Church's institutions and attitudes must similarly be updated to make them compatible with a world characterized by constant and progressively more rapid change. By doing this, the Church will come to grips with what it has always proclaimed as the purpose for which it was founded, to bring the good news of salvation to all men. Such was the essence of the Johannine dream of a fruitful collaboration of the Church and the world in the common task of bringing man to the fullness of his destiny.

Index

The Author

Gary MacEoin has had thirty years experience as a journalist, writer, and editor, and for many years he has represented the International Catholic Press Union at the United Nations. He covered the second and fourth sessions of the Second Vatican Council for over twenty-five newspapers in the United States and Canada.

Mr. MacEoin was born in a village of twenty homes in County Sligo, western Ireland. He received an A.B. degree from the University of London in 1941, and then did graduate work at the National University of Ireland, receiving a Master's degree in 1942 and a Ph.D. in 1951. In 1943 he was admitted to the bar in Ireland.

After reporting for the *Irish Press* and the *Irish Independent* in Dublin, Mr. MacEoin went to Trinidad in 1944 as editor of the *Port-of-Spain Gazette*. After three years, he became Director of Information for the Caribbean Commission, and then came to New York City in 1949 as Sunday editor of the Spanish-language newspaper *La Prensa*. Gary MacEoin has served as editor for several Spanish-language journals, among them *La Hacienda*, a Spanish agricultural monthly, which he edited for twelve years. He wrote the script for a Voice of America weekly broadcast to Latin America for five years. In 1963 he supervised production of a documentary film on the Peace Corps in Colombia.

Mr. MacEoin travels constantly. In the past twenty-seven months he has been out of the United States for eighteen, visiting eight European, fourteen African, twelve Asian, and ten Latin American countries. He has lectured on Latin America at many U.S. universities, including Swarthmore, Fordham, and San Francisco State. His previous books include *Nothing Is Quite Enough; Latin America: The Eleventh Hour; New Challenges to American Catholics;* and *Colombia, Venezuela, the Guianas.*